THE STORY OF

Ridgeons

A 100-Year Journey

1911–2011

THE STORY OF
Ridgeons
A 100-Year Journey

NIGEL WATSON

ISBN 978 1 906507 22 0

First published in 2011
by James & James (Publishers) Ltd
a member of Third Millennium Information
2–5 Benjamin Street
London
EC1M 5QL

www.tmiltd.com

JAMES
X
JAMES

Project management and design by Vimbai Shire
Production by Bonnie Murray
Modern photography by Charles Best and Hiroshi Shimura
Reprographics by Studio Fasoli, Italy
Printed by Gorenjksi Tisk, Slovenia

Picture Acknowledgements

The bulk of the illustrations come from the Ridgeons' archives and the collections of individual staff and family members. The Publishers would like to thank all those who have contributed images and, in particular, Fiona Parish at The Cambridge Library, for her expert advice and help throughout the project and all Ridgeons' staff who have contributed material and given generously of their time. The Publishers would also like to thank the following agencies and individuals for permission to reproduce material: Alamy 24 (middle right and bottom); Hiroshi Shimura 15 (bottom), 24 (bottom left), 33 (top), 51, 52, (top), 63; (middle right); National Science & Society Picture Library 46 (top left, middle left and right), 48 (middle); RIBA Library Drawings Collection 14 (bottom left); The Cambridge Collection 15 (top), 16 (top), 17 (bottom left, top right), 22 (all images), 32, 32–33 (bottom), 36 (top), 37 (middle), 45 (top), 48 (top), 78 (bottom left); the Robert Tressell Society 18 (top left); Tony Green 14 (middle, left and right).

Jacket, front: Ridgeons lorry making deliveries near King's College, Cambridge. Back, main picture: Aerial view of the first Ridgeons site at Tenison Road. Small pictures, clockwise from top left: The founder of Ridgeons, Cyril Ridgeon; Long Service Awards, 2010; Cheque presenation to the East Ambulance Air Ambulace crew Halesworth branch; Counter service, Nuffield Road with (from left) Alan Eve and Nick Farr.
Half title: Line drawing of horse and cart outside the original Tenison Road premises, c.1915.
Title page: Cyril Ridgeon and staff with his fleet of lorries,1930. The company's first lorry, the Wolverine, can be seen (third vehicle from left) as can the Daimler (fourth vehicle from left). The staff members are, from right: Elliot Ridgeon, Cyril Ridgeon, Victor Keys, Leslie Ridgeon, Howard Jarman, Percy Moule, Bill Cullum, Johnny Naylor, Dick Rolph and Len Bigmore.
Page 7: Ridgeons delivery note.
Page 9: Centenary garden, with landscaping display by Gus Chichon and team.

Contents

Acknowledgements

IT HAS BEEN A PLEASURE discovering the history of Ridgeons, especially hearing the reminiscences of some of the people who have helped the company to retain its sense of family identity in a world dominated by major corporate brands. After a century of success, the story of Ridgeons is testament to the strength and contribution of the family business in the British economy. It highlights the importance of values based not only on profit but also on care, concern and compassion for all those who make businesses living organisations. Such values have recently become fashionable again, with recent research claiming to have rediscovered them. In fact, they have never gone away, for businesses like Ridgeons have been practising these values consistently for generations. In showing that they can be sustained within a growing organisation, they offer an important lesson for other businesses today.

I was made to feel welcome whomever I met and wherever I went. I would particularly like to thank Anne Ridgeon and Gordon Ridgeon for their guidance and advice and Fiona Viney for her unfailingly good-humoured help with all the administrative arrangements. The text would have been much poorer without the often vivid contributions from so many people connected with the company whom I have had the pleasure of interviewing over a period of months. In addition, the book *Cyril Ridgeon & Son Ltd – In and around Cambridge, 1911–1976* by Ivor Warren, which covered the early years of the business, proved to be an invaluable resource for this history.

NIGEL WATSON
June 2010

Foreword

AS MY FATHER DAVID often says, 'It is always important to mark an occasion!' On reaching 100 years, we felt the opportunity could not pass without a book that captured not only the journey of the company but, importantly, recognised as many people as possible who have contributed to the changing story of our business. In so saying, this book is dedicated to our members of staff and, on a personal footing, to my father, who has had the vision and dedication to lead the business for 50 years until 2002.

This book serves as both a thanksgiving and a celebration. It offers an opportunity to sincerely thank our own people as well as customers and suppliers for their support and loyalty – in instances over generations – and without whom Ridgeons would not be here.

We also celebrate that, despite all the challenges and changes to which this book holds testament, we have survived to tell the tale at all! 'Adapt or die' is one of the basic tenets of evolution theory. My father's version of this is 'stand still and you go backwards', and, over the years, we have always looked to improve what we do but never in a way that jeopardises our principles of 'how we do business'. We fervently strive to retain and demonstrate these values and principles in all our dealings with each other and our customers, as lived within the business in our great-grandfather's day.

Our thanks go to Nigel Watson, our author, who has done a remarkable job in weaving the strands of our evolving tale together and placing them so expertly within the social and economic era of the day. His thorough, scholarly and sensitive approach, not least in dealing with the huge number of interviews conducted as part of his research – as well as handling with such apparent unyielding vigour and enthusiasm the sixty archive cardboard boxes presented to him – has produced a book which we trust will be both interesting and entertaining to read.

I wish also to thank my cousin, Gordon Ridgeon, who, together with Sue Schneider, Jane Wakelin and Pat Coxhill, has created such an extensive and comprehensive archive.

We hope you enjoy learning more about the trials, successes and personalities that created the Ridgeon Group over the last 100 years. I know much pleasure has been derived by those involved in reliving and sharing their memories with Nigel and I hope we can now share this enjoyment with you.

ANNE RIDGEON
Chairman
Ridgeon Group
June 2010

The Early Years
1911–28

1

THE RIDGEON GROUP is one of the largest independent builders' merchants in the UK. It is still owned by the founding family, with the fourth generation active in the management of the business. Operating from 21 branches, it has carved out a position as the leading builders' merchant in East Anglia. The ethos established by the founder, Cyril Ridgeon, based on honesty, integrity and fairness and developed by successive generations of the family, still defines the character of the business and its relationship with employees, customers and suppliers.

Above: Cyril Ridgeon.

Facing page: The picturesque village of Hartest, Suffolk, where Ridgeons' founder Cyril Ridgeon was born.

Previous pages: Punting along the River Cam, with Clare College in the background. As a thriving university town, Cambridge has provided ample opportunities for the construction industry. Ridgeons has supplied a range of building materials to colleges over the years.

The story begins with Cyril Ridgeon. He was born in the small Suffolk village of Hartest, not far from Bury St Edmunds, in 1873. His grandfather had been the village publican, and his father, Charles, was running the village pub, The Victoria. But Charles Ridgeon had been apprenticed as a stonemason – he helped to carry out repairs to Lavenham's medieval church – and he was working as a mason once more when the family moved to Cambridge in the early 1890s. It seemed unlikely that Cyril would follow his father into construction for he was employed as a clerk on the railway when he was 18. It was his younger brother, Robert, aged 16, who took up their father's trade. There were three more brothers, William, the eldest, born in 1871, Horace, born in 1880, and Ernest, born in 1884. Horace too would become a mason.

Above, left and right: The Victoria public house, Thurston, which still displays its original signage (above right). Cyril's grandfather, William Ridgeon, is listed in its records as landlord between 1844 and 1874. Cyril's father, Charles Ridgeon, ran the pub for a time before resuming his original trade as a stonemason. Charles moved his family to Hartest (top), a small village near Bury St Edmunds, just before Cyril was born in 1873.

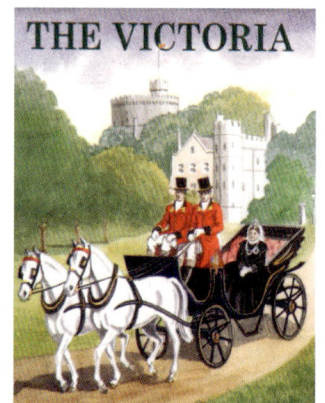

Left: Watercolour of the interior of the St Peter and St Paul Parish Church, Lavenham, painted by Aston Webb in 1873. Cyril's father, Charles Ridgeon, helped to carry out repairs to this church as part of his work as a stonemason. This would have been a mammoth task as the cracked plasterwork, the discoloured stonework and the warped roof timbers illustrated in this painting show.

At the end of the 19th century Cambridge was undergoing something of a revival. The university, the core of the town, was flourishing, with the foundation of several new colleges; the government of the town had been reformed; and by 1900 its population had risen to just over 38,000. For workers involved in construction, there was plenty of work in Cambridge, not just from the university, but also from steadily expanding suburban development. This reflected the national trend, for the decade from the mid-1890s onwards saw the last building boom before the First World War. Between 1891 and 1901 an annual national average of 147,000 houses was built.

Cyril Ridgeon did not last long as a railway clerk. In 1891 he joined the staff of a brick and tile manufacturer, Watts and Son, based in Newmarket Road, Cambridge. This work he found much more to his liking, and six years later, he moved to a firm of timber importers, Bristow & Copley of King's Lynn, as their sales representative for the eastern counties. By then he had married Beatrice Johnson, known as Trix, who came from Isleham. Cyril also began representing the Cam Portland Cement Company, based in the village of Meldreth, a few miles southwest of Cambridge. A whole series of small notebooks survives,

Above: Cyril Ridgeon, his wife Beatrice, 'Trix', and a young Elliot, c.1917.

The end of the 19th century saw massive growth in construction in and around Cambridge, including the university. Newnham College (left) was one of the colleges built during this time. Founded in 1871, the original site housed five female students at 74 Regent Street, Cambridge. The first building (now called Old Hall, far left) was built on this site on Sidgwick Avenue in 1875. Three more buildings, including the dining hall (shown right), were built to expand the college between 1875 and 1910.

Above: Watts and Son, the brick and tile manufacturer in Newmarket Road, where Cyril worked from 1891 to 1897.

Below: Hand-written pages from a selection of Cyril Ridgeon's notebooks from his time as sales representative for timber importers Bristow & Copley, King's Lynn.

stamped with Cyril Ridgeon's name and address, listing timber imports from the Baltic and North America.

He carried on with this work for ten years. Then in 1911 he fell ill. It must have been serious for he spent several months in a nursing home, although the nature of his illness remains unknown. He was never really in very good health for the rest of his life, but the strength of his determination more than made up for his physical frailty. Confinement to bed gave him plenty of time to think about his future, and he eventually decided he would set up in business on his own account. The firm, which became the largest family-owned group of builders' merchants in the country, began in the back bedroom of Cyril's modest house at 44 St Barnabas Road, Cambridge, in November 1911. Initially Cyril acted as an agent on behalf of his previous employers, Watts and Son, Bristow & Copley and the Cam Portland Cement Company. He later remembered how 'the builders of Cambridge were very kind' in giving him their orders, although such modesty hides the fact that Cyril Ridgeon was a very good salesman. In those early days he travelled by train and bicycle to visit his customers in and around Cambridge. For instance, he would alight at Newmarket and then cycle round to customers in Fordham, Burwell and the

Left: Cyril's former home in St Barnabas Road, Cambridge, where he began operating his business from an office in the back bedroom of this house.

Below left: High Street, Newmarket, and Commercial Road, Swaffham (below), c.1900. Cyril would probably have cycled along these streets many times, calling on local customers.

boy and yardman; I was boss, traveller and assistant to Mr C when in the office'.

Cyril's timing in starting up his own business was opportune. The construction industry was just beginning to recover from a depression stretching back to the early 1900s, when restrictions on credit were imposed after the heavy cost of the Boer War. Life for many builders was difficult because there was so much competition. With the industry composed of countless small firms (before 1914 the average building firm employed fewer than ten workers), it was easy for newcomers to set up in business. By 1909 unemployment in the building industry was at its worst since 1881. The rate of unemployment among carpenters and plumbers rose from 8 per cent in 1905 to 12 per cent in 1909. Matters were made worse by technical changes, especially the introduction of reinforced concrete and woodworking machinery, which reduced job opportunities. Labourers suffered most. Earning only 70 per cent of a craftsman's wage, they were always the first to be sacked in a slump. The misery that many endured was eloquently portrayed in the book *The Ragged Trousered*

Swaffhams before returning to Cambridge by train from Swaffham Prior. Spending so much time out and about, Cyril quickly recognised that he needed help in the office. In April 1912 he took on his first employee, Bill Cornell, who remained with the firm until his death in 1955. Cyril would later describe how Cornell acted as 'general manager, office

Robert Tressell was the author of *The Ragged Trousered Philanthropists*, published in 1914 and based largely on his experiences of working as signwriter and decorator. The popularity of the story has led to numerous reprints of the book, several stage adaptations and an annual festival held in Tressell's memory by the Robert Tressell Society. This picture (above) shows the society's banner.

While working for one of these builders, Kerridge & Shaw, he began running errands for his uncle after work. He became one of the mainstays of the business, eventually retiring in 1961. Leslie's arrival gave Cyril, he later recalled, more time 'to hunt up orders'. Another newcomer who joined around the same time was Bill Cullum, later a lorry driver.

When the railways were the main carriers of freight around the country, many businesses began life in or close to railway goods yards. At Tenison Road the trains of the Great Eastern Railway brought in timber as well as chimney pots, drain pipes and slates, all scattered around the yard. Irish workers hired on piece rates unloaded the timber from the rail trucks into a shed by hand, walking down a single scaffold board. A handcart was used to deliver goods to

Philanthropists, published in 1914 and written by Robert Tressell, himself a house painter.

For his first two years Cyril acted only as an agent for other firms, but his success, combined with his experience and knowledge of building materials, encouraged him to think about establishing his own yard and stocking his own goods. In 1913 he rented from the Great Eastern Railway a small area adjacent to their Tenison Road goods yard in Cambridge. He put up a small hut as an office and took on his second member of staff, his 16-year-old nephew Leslie, son of his eldest brother William. Finishing school at 14, the leaving age in those days, Leslie trained with a local firm of ironmongers and hardware merchants, Macintosh & Sons. After a short spell working for a firm of scientific instrument makers, he worked for two local builders as a draughtsman.

Top: Line drawing of Cyril Ridgeon's premises at Tenison Road, 1911. Materials were hand delivered, with larger orders fulfilled by horse and cart.

Above left: Bill Cornell, the first Ridgeons employee, who worked for the company right up to the time of his death in 1955.

Above right: Bill Cullum, the firm's first lorry driver.

Facing page: Aerial view of the first Ridgeons site at Tenison Road. Although this picture was taken in 1962, it shows the extent of the site and its proximity to the railway.

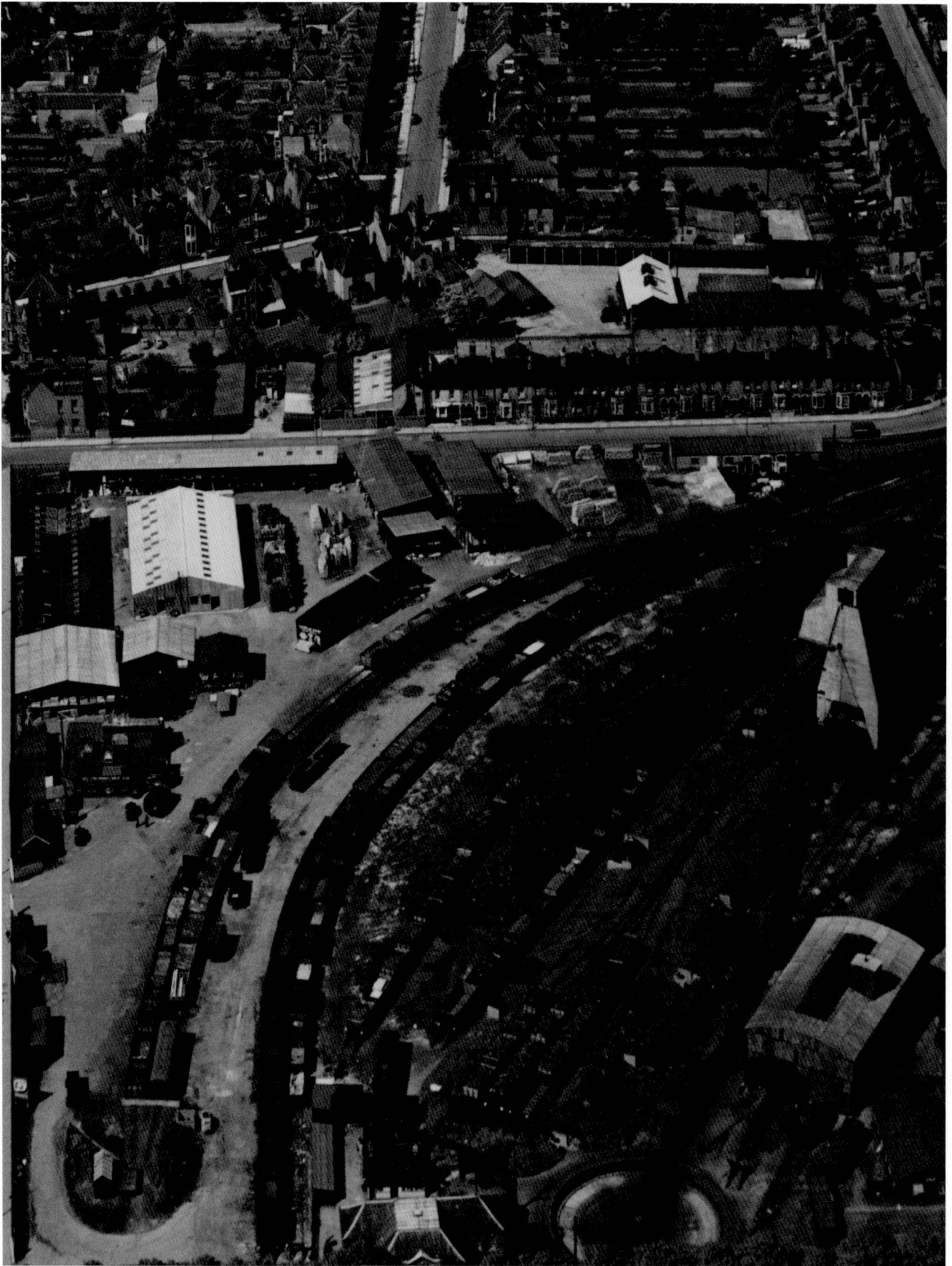

local customers while a horse and cart was hired for those farther away. Cyril Ridgeon and his small staff regularly worked 12-hour days. Leslie Ridgeon later remembered how Cyril would arrive at Tenison Road at 7.30 a.m. then set off with his bicycle to catch the train and do his rounds, returning to the yard between five and six in the evening.

Merchants dealing in a wide variety of construction materials were still uncommon. The local directory for Cambridge published in 1913 has no separate heading for builders' merchants. This appears for the first time in the 1916 directory, listing just six for the whole of Cambridgeshire, of which only two, Cyril Ridgeon and H&A Swan Bros Ltd, of East Road, were in Cambridge itself. Swan Brothers had first appeared in the 1913 directory as brick and tile merchants. Directories for the 1860s give comprehensive coverage of the construction industry, listing brick and tile makers, brick merchants, builders, carpenters and joiners, manufacturing joiners and contractors, creosoting works, iron merchants and ironmongers, plumbers and glaziers, lime merchants and sand merchants, millwrights and sawmills, timber merchants and dealers – but there is not a single reference to a builders' merchant. By the late 1870s, a listing had appeared for building material dealers, but just one was listed, in Soham. Builders' merchants appear for the first time alongside building material dealers in the 1890s. The combination of urban growth and the extensive railway network made it possible for merchants to stock a wide array of related goods and make them easily available to customers.

This page: Timber stacks past (above) and present (left, top and bottom). Timber piles in the old days could be stacked as high as 60 feet – impressive considering it was all done by hand. Notable concessions to current health and safety legislation in the modern pictures include the level concrete ground, workmen in safety jackets and gloves, and lower timber stacks stored on specially constructed steel racking. Mechanical handling has taken over the backbreaking work of loading the racks by hand, with forklift trucks being used to move the stacks.

Any plans Cyril Ridgeon might have had for the business were shattered by the coming of the First World War in August 1914. Leslie Ridgeon remembered how troops destined for the British Expeditionary Force embarked on their trains at the Tenison Road station. Some of them asked for a tap for water to brew tea and, as they were leaving, one of them nailed a ration biscuit to the outside of the shed. It was still there when Leslie returned from war service in 1919. Throughout the conflict the sidings at Tenison Road were busy with military traffic, from horses and guns to wagons and other equipment. Troop trains passed through the station while ambulance trains brought back the wounded to the First Eastern Hospital, a series of huts set up along the Backs.

Clockwise from top: Military activity, such as this convoy pictured on Cherry Hinton Road in 1914, became a common sight on the streets of Cambridge during the war; A Cambridgeshire regiment leaving for an unknown destination, 1914; Ward Nine of the First Eastern Hospital, a military hospital established by the Royal Army Medical Corps to treat wounded soldiers, and erected in a series of huts along the Backs.

Members of the North Staffordshire Regiment bathe in the River Cam, August 1914. Rows of tents which form their camp can be seen in the background.

Cyril Ridgeon later recollected the impact of the war on his infant venture:

> Then came the war and I thought ruin. I was staggered and expected my business to tumble about my ears like a pack of cards. After a few days of extreme depression I pulled myself together and began to look after firms that had Government contracts. I started in the English timber trade – bought trees, sold them to Government Contractors as far away as Birmingham etc, sold them to Builders in Cambridge, and persuaded them to make crates to Government specifications for Government food contractors. The contractors sent me cheques with orders for crates and begged for urgent deliveries. All this was done under Government Controls and the margin of profit was extremely small but the quantities were large.

With repairs, maintenance and alterations, this work kept many other construction firms afloat all over the country after almost all building work had ground to a halt. Another challenge was the shortage of labour caused by the call up of so many men for military service. Both Leslie Ridgeon and Bill Cornell entered the army. Leslie was under age

when he joined the Suffolk Yeomanry and eventually fought with the Argyll & Sutherland Highlanders in the Dardanelles and Salonika. In their absence, Cyril did receive a welcome helping hand from his two stonemason brothers, Robert and Horace, while he used sub-contractors to manage the volume of orders he received. He still cycled around the local villages, taking orders for ammunition boxes. An early invoice survives from 1915, listing a delivery of 4,000 pressed bricks at a load price of £4 12s to Mr C.W. Unwin in nearby Histon. By the second half of the war the business had sales of around £30,000 a year, worth about £1.2m today, based on increases in the retail price index (RPI). On the other hand, profits were relatively small, between £1,000 and £2,000 a year.

When his nephew and Bill Cornell came back from the war in 1919, Cyril organised a small celebration, making a speech and presenting them with the accumulated sum he had set aside each week for them during their absence. Leslie came back thankful to be alive and determined that no one who fell under his charge should ever be found guilty of wasting time. He had been bayoneted during the war, surviving only because he had fatally bayoneted his attacker in return. In his later years he would become known for his brusque instruction, 'Come on, boy!' and his inability to suffer fools gladly.

With the return of Leslie Ridgeon and Bill Cornell, recalled Cyril later, 'we had to start all over again'. Once labour was freely available, several new sheds were erected at Tenison Road, storing timber purchased from the state, which still controlled supplies. Then came the boom in prices as demand suppressed during the war exploded. For Cyril Ridgeon, the benefit came from the escalating prices of building materials, of which so little had been produced during the war. In 1918 only one-third of the pre-war volume of bricks and light castings was made, there was only half as much cement, and the production of roofing tiles stood at just 6 per cent of pre-war levels. The rapid peacetime removal of wartime controls led to rapid price rises, aggravated by the huge post-war housing programme. Too few materials were in too much demand. By 1920 prices were more than three times their pre-war level. Turnover shot up, although the rate of inflation meant that revenue of £48,000 in 1920, more than 50 per cent higher than in 1918, was the modern equivalent of £1.5m, only just over a quarter higher in real terms. In contrast, the firm's profits of £8,000, almost 20 per cent of turnover, were almost six times higher in real terms. Cyril's staff shared in

Left: A young Leslie Ridgeon in uniform.

Above: An early Ridgeons invoice dated October 1915 to Mr C.W. Unwin in Histon.

this good fortune, for he was always appreciative of the work done by those he employed and had begun paying annual bonuses linked to profits as soon as the war ended. He also welcomed the introduction of the eight-hour working day soon after the war ended, remarking that 'if strenuously carried out [this] is enough for one day's work'. All this was typical of his approach towards the people he employed, which owed much to Cyril's strong Christian faith. For many years he was deacon and secretary of St Andrew's Street Baptist Church in Cambridge, a link retained by successive generations of the family. They would also perpetuate his approach towards the company's staff and their welfare. It was Cyril who began the tradition of annual staff outings, which lasted until rising numbers eventually made such an event impracticable. The first occurred in July 1922, when staff members were taken to the Royal Show in Cambridge. In 1925 there was a visit to London by train to see the Empire Exhibition, where one of the firm's customers, Kerridge's, had worked on one of the pavilions. In the same year the firm celebrated both the coming of age of Cyril's only son, Cyril Elliot Ridgeon, known as Elliot, and his entry into the firm, following his student days at Trinity Hall, Cambridge, from where he gained his degree in economics, after studying under the great John Maynard Keynes. Another visit took place to the Royal Show in 1926.

The profits recorded in 1920–1 would not be surpassed until the Second World War. On the other hand, given the very variable economic climate of the 1920s, Cyril Ridgeon's business never once made a loss. After the slump which followed the boom, turnover rose steadily and profits remained relatively respectable. This was partly because the climate for construction improved, as shortages of labour and materials disappeared and costs fell. The firm was becoming better known. It was employing more staff, stocking more goods and acquiring more plant.

The pattern for long service, which became characteristic of the business, was already being established. Sid Stone joined in 1919, later becoming yard foreman, and remained with the firm until his retirement in 1971. His brother, Joe, came in 1921. Rather deaf from gunnery service during the war, he developed his own inimitable trade vocabulary. In 1922 John Rivers was recruited as a junior bookkeeper. A warm, kind man, he later qualified and became the company accountant, retiring in 1968. Howard Jarman was just 16 when he joined the firm in 1923, serving more than 50 years as a yardman, storeman, driver and manager of the

ironmongery department. He was known for his very neat handwriting. Another newcomer was Dave Langley, who came in 1924 and retired in 1946 aged 77. He was known for his droll sense of humour and his idiosyncratic expressions: anything that annoyed him, for instance, was 'noserating'. Although he was only a small man, he was quite capable of shifting bags of cement weighing two hundredweight (100kg). He never wore a coat, regardless of the weather, so could often be found, jacket steaming, drying out in front of a stove. He also looked after the horse that pulled the delivery cart. In the office, women were employed for the first time, the initial four being Miss Hilda Cresswell, Miss Francis, Miss Freda Jobson and Miss Joan Pearson. Miss Pearson would later recall how Cyril Ridgeon was accompanied to the office each day by his white-and-tan terrier, Bonzo, who 'was slightly snappy and so was treated with respect'.

Above: The Great Exhibition, held in a purpose-built site in Wembley in 1924–5 was a huge display of goods and produce from the Empire countries of the time and was one of the first destinations of many annual outings taken by the Ridgeons staff. Visitor attractions at the exhibition included an amusement park, a stadium for mass entertainments, and a boating lake.

Above: Trinity Hall, Cambridge, where Elliot Ridgeon studied economics.

Above: Official guide programme for the exhibition.

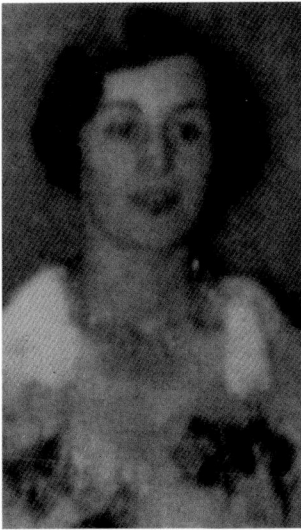

Above: Hilda Cresswell, a typist, was the first woman employed by Ridgeons.

Above: Cyril's dog Bonzo was a regular visitor to the offices at Tenison Road.

Cyril Ridgeon bought the firm's first lorry in 1922. After the war haulage firms began springing up all over the country, often started by ex-servicemen utilising former military vehicles, and for the first time they provided real competition to the railways for the carriage of freight. Ridgeons' first lorry was a US government surplus Wolverine, which had never been unpacked. A few years later Cyril described the vehicle as 'a jibber' that had to be treated tenderly – 'If it were overloaded, it couldn't be moved because the load had put the brakes on.' Bill Cullum was taken on as the first driver. Developing the vehicle fleet became one of Leslie Ridgeon's responsibilities. The Wolverine was followed by a three-ton solid-tyre Daimler in 1926, and a five-ton Leyland, converted from a bus chassis, in 1928. A second driver, Victor Keys, was recruited. A collection of notebooks from the 1920s recording haulage rates shows the firm was delivering materials all over East Anglia.

While Leslie Ridgeon carried on travelling, cycling around Cambridge collecting orders from customers, Bill Cornell was appointed as the firm's first formal sales representative in 1922. A year later he was given a Diamond motorcycle to speed up his journeys between customers.

There were new products to stock, such as laminated paper board, known as Essex Board, and Celotex, made from sugar cane fibre and hardboard, as well as asbestos sheets and plasterboard. More plywood was ordered in response to growing demand. There were new plastering materials and metal window frames. Many of these products were devised in response to the shortage of more traditional materials immediately after the war. Timber was becoming an even larger part of the firm's business, delivered from various ports, including King's Lynn, but principally from the Surrey Commercial Docks in London, the UK's leading timber port. The firm sold a great variety of timber – there was pine from British Columbia, American black walnut and whitewood, African whitewood or obechi, English and Australian walnut and Iroko teak.

In 1925, when Cyril's son, Elliot, became a partner in the firm, the business changed its name to Cyril Ridgeon & Son. His father was delighted at his son's arrival for his health was suffering once more – 'I was getting rather spun out and [Elliot] took over the office and relieved me of everything with the exception of the Timber portion'. Elliot Ridgeon would be the guiding light of the business for almost half a century.

Right: Cyril Ridgeon and staff with his fleet of lorries,1930. The company's first lorry, the Wolverine can be seen (third vehicle from left) as can the Daimler (fourth vehicle from left). From right: Elliot Ridgeon, Cyril Ridgeon, Victor Keys, Leslie Ridgeon, Howard Jarman, Percy Moule, Bill Cullum, Johnny Naylor, Dick Rolph and Len Bigmore.

The Builders' Encyclopaedia 1928–39

2

Facing page: Customers and staff on the shop floor of the Nuffield Road branch, Cambridge. Building loyal relationships between staff, customers and suppliers has been an important part of Ridgeons' ethos from the **outset.**

Above: Trade display windows facing Tenison Road.

Previous pages: Timber frame roof using Ridgeons' trusses.

FATHER AND SON made a good team, overseeing the growth of the business and expanding what it offered to customers, during the worst trade depression on record. It was during this period that the firm began to develop its distinctive commitment to customer service, based on an extensive product range and the knowledge of staff, which still mark out the business today.

Cyril Ridgeon remained responsible for timber, something that was always his first love. When he saw how local rivals were setting up their own timber mills, he decided the best way to respond was to do exactly the same.

Top: Railway sidings at Tenison Road. Cyril's brother, Horace Ridgeon, used to quip that timber in the early days came into the yard 'mixed up like chocolate in a box'. The job of sorting and stacking the timber in the days prior to mechanical handling (above) was labour-intensive, back-breaking work.

In 1928 land was acquired in Cavendish Road, on the other side of the railway line from Tenison Road. A railway siding was built during 1928–9 at a cost to the firm of £506. It ran in a loop from the existing Coldham Lane sidings by the London & North Eastern Railway – the successor to the Great Eastern – and began operating on 27 May 1929. Storage sheds were built, some of them second-hand from Marshall's aerodrome, and a sawmill laid down. Much of the work was delegated to Cyril's brother, Robert, but Ernest Maxim, an experienced mill manager appointed in 1929, oversaw the installation of the sawmill. Among the mill machinery was a Ruston Hornsby engine, costing £960, a five-cutter, planer, spindle moulder and several saws. Robert Ridgeon became manager of the new depot while brother Horace took over as yard foreman at Tenison Road.

Transferring the firm's timber operations to the new site made much more space available for building materials at Tenison Road. Some timber was still stocked there, as Ivor Warren recorded in his previous history of the firm, 'particularly for the small builders and carpenters who wished to collect by handcart and were not prepared for the onerous task of negotiating the steep slope of Mill Road Bridge'.

Left: Storage sheds at Cavendish Road, c.1930, showing (bottom left of the picture) uncut, untreated logs and (far left and in sheds) the cut timber sorted and stacked. The storage sheds protected the timber from becoming water damaged when it rained. Piling the timber in high stacks out in the open was still standard practice throughout the timber industry in the 1930s, so the sheds were an innovative addition to the site.

Above: This Ruston Hornsby engine formed part of the mill machinery driving all the machines by belt at Cavendish Road.

Right: Aerial view of the Cavendish Road site.

All this investment was taking place just as the building trade began to suffer from the impact of the slump. This caused serious unemployment, with almost a third of all insured building workers out of work in 1932. Even five years later, the total was 15 per cent. Yet construction as a whole proved much more resilient than many other sectors of industry. It was helped by the falling costs of construction, a phenomenon which lasted until the mid-1930s, cheap credit and the expansion of the building societies and limited planning controls, all of which contributed towards a surge in demand for housing during the 1930s. Houses had never been so cheap. It was calculated that a man on the average industrial wage required the earnings from working only two and a half years to purchase a house. Between 1929 and 1938 half of all domestic investment in the UK went into new housing. In the 14 years between 1919 and 1933 private enterprise constructed 1.3m new homes; in the six years from 1934 to 1938 this figure reached 1.4m.

Cambridge proved no different from the rest of the UK, as the firm's results showed. Profits throughout the 1930s averaged a respectable 7 per cent of turnover. New houses sprang up all over the town, from mass housing estates to the large houses along Girton, Madingley and Trumpington Roads. Among the latter was Latham House, built for Elliot Ridgeon in 1930, and 292 Hill Road, built for Cyril and Beatrice in 1924; Cyril and Elliot also invested in a group of houses built along Milton Road, beyond the new Kings Hedges and Green End Roads, and in flats at Grange Gardens, off Grange Road. All this activity stimulated a huge demand for bricks, and the firm supplied untold quantities

to most of the well-established local firms as well as many smaller ones which had sprung up to take advantage of the boom. The latter still dominated the industry. In 1930 84 per cent of building firms employed ten employees or fewer. Five years later there were still fewer than 1,000 firms out of a total of 73,000 capable of building 100 or more houses every year. With few economies of scale, smaller firms could operate just as effectively as larger firms, although they were much more vulnerable in bad times. Making up the bulk of Cyril Ridgeon & Son's customers, small firms would have relied on extended credit from the firm. One such business was run by Harold Ridgeon, another nephew working for Cyril, who had completed his academic studies at St Catharine's College where, as a commoner, he paid for himself and achieved first class honours in economics and achieved a BA in June 1929. He continued his education in the building trade under his uncle and he was later encouraged to set up on his own. He

Above: Harold Ridgeon, Cyril's nephew, was employed at Ridgeons after his studies at St Catharine's College (top). He later set up on his own, running several successful business ventures, including a building firm, a grocery store, several farms and an abattoir.

Above: Cyril Ridgeon (left) and son Elliot (right), 1930. Father and son were smart gentlemen, and their trade in the timber business did not stop them from reporting daily for work in their suits and trilby hats.

Facing page, above and left: The 1930s boom saw a rise in housing construction across Cambridge. Houses being built at the start of the housing boom in Milton Road, 1927.

Right: The Ridgeon family tree, showing Cyril Ridgeon's descendants.

This page, clockwise from top left: A young David Ridgeon with Daphne Byrt, a family friend, and their pet dogs; David Ridgeon at his wedding to Jill Starling in 1961; David Ridgeon (left) and Patricia Brooksbank (née Ridgeon (second from right) and Michael Ridgeon (right) with their mother, Mrs Joan Ridgeon (centre), 1985.

Opposite, clockwise from top left: Cyril and Beatrix Ridgeon with their young grandson David on holiday, c.1932; Three generations of the Ridgeon family in the garden of Latham House, their home in Trumpington Road. From left, back row: Elliot Ridgeon, Joan Ridgeon, Beatrix Ridgeon and Cyril Ridgeon. At front: Michael and David Ridgeon; Elliot Ridgeon enjoying a game of croquet with David and Michael Ridgeon; Joan Ridgeon with (from left) a family friend, Michael and David Ridgeon; Michael Ridgeon weds Penny Powell; A young Gordon Ridgeon pushing his cousin Rachel on her toy horse, 1964; Gordon pictured many years later with his eldest son Thomas, at the East Barnwell Community Centre, where Ridgeons donated tools and materials for a 'facelift day', 2001.

would become very successful and later take over and expand one of the most respected and long established building firms in Cambridge, William Sindall. He was joined by his brother Frank Ridgeon and together they drove William Sindall forward to national significance and a listing on the Birmingham Stock Exchange in 1965. His other business ventures included Adkins, the grocers, the Gonville Hotel in Cambridge, farms at Abington and Hengrave, near Bury St Edmunds, and a meat processing business in Cherry Hinton.

Builders' merchants were expected to collect bricks directly from brickworks and deliver them on site. The lorries belonging to Cyril Ridgeon & Son travelled regularly to and from the Fletton Brick Company at Peterborough and London Brick at Warboys, near Huntingdon, carrying 2,500 and 4,000 bricks per load respectively. It was slow work. One delivery from London Brick, with an industrial tractor and trailer travelling at 10 miles an hour, was supposed to take a day to complete but the driver, Fred Bigmore, and his mate would start very early and carry out three deliveries every two days. To meet demand, the firm also used local hauliers, but there were plenty of them around. With so much competition, their rates were cheap but they were not always very reliable. With competition among hauliers encouraging overloading and minimal maintenance, breakdowns were common, and it was not unusual for irate foremen to telephone the firm demanding to know where the bricks were that they so urgently needed.

The Ridgeon Family Tree

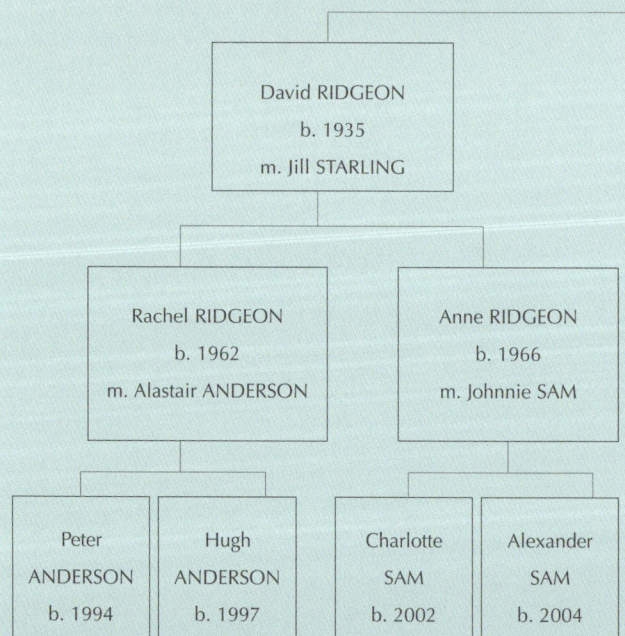

David RIDGEON
b. 1935
m. Jill STARLING

Rachel RIDGEON
b. 1962
m. Alastair ANDERSON

Anne RIDGEON
b. 1966
m. Johnnie SAM

Peter
ANDERSON
b. 1994

Hugh
ANDERSON
b. 1997

Charlotte
SAM
b. 2002

Alexander
SAM
b. 2004

Cyril RIDGEON
1873–1942

Beatrix JOHNSON
1874–1966

Elliot RIDGEON
1904–1973
m. Joan MILLER

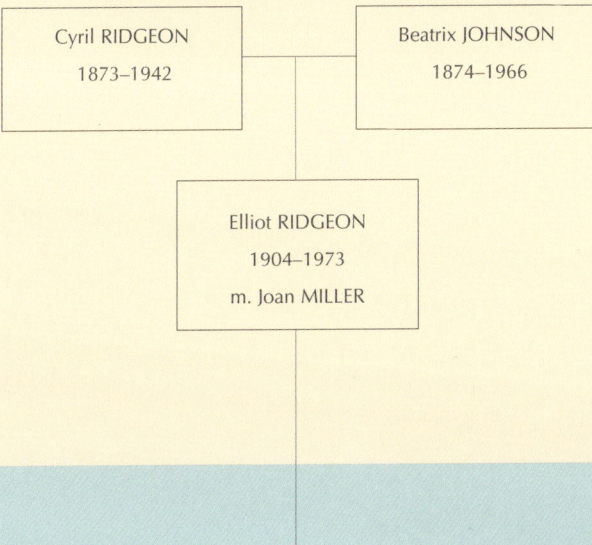

Michael RIDGEON
b. 1937
m. Penny Powell

John RIDGEON
Feb 1942–Feb 1942

Patricia RIDGEON
b. 1944
m. John BROOKSBANK

Gordon RIDGEON
b. 1962
m. Gillian ABSALOM

Duncan RIDGEON
b. 1964
m. Pauline MERISON

Amanda RIDGEON
b. 1969
m. Glenn SMITH

Philip BROOKSBANK
b. 1974
m. Shu HONG

Andrew BROOKSBANK
b. 1975

Thomas
RIDGEON
b. 1995

William
RIDGEON
b. 1998

Daniel
RIDGEON
b. 1993

Naomi
RIDGEON
b. 1996

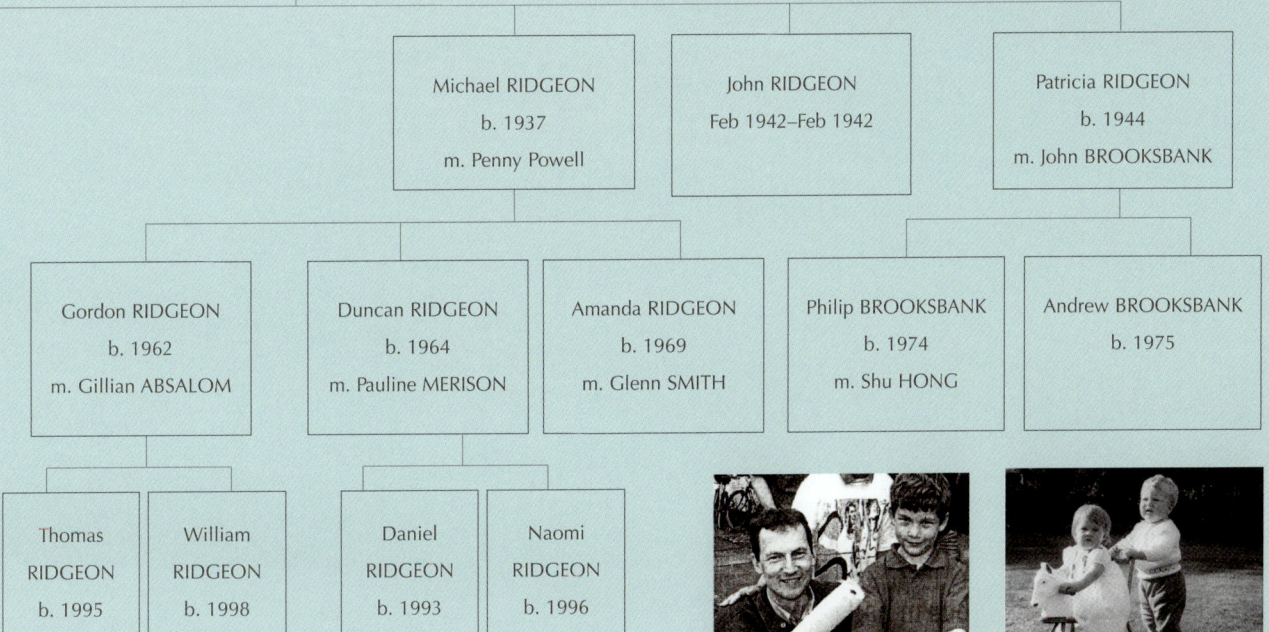

Public authorities were also busy building. The university built a new library and the County Council constructed its first village college. As the rearmament programme later got underway, existing local aerodromes, such as Duxford, were modernised, and new ones, including Debden, Bassingbourn and Wyton, were built. When the firm was supplying bricks for the new school being built in Bateson Road in Chesterton, the contractor asked if the firm could help to accelerate progress by delivering 100,000 bricks in one day. Given that a maximum load contained 3,000 bricks, every one of which had to be loaded and unloaded by hand, this was a huge task. The firm rose to the challenge, organising local hauliers and seeking help from London Brick while the building contractors hired extra men. It turned out that deliveries spilled over into a second day, by which time the

Top: Construction of Cambridge University Library, 1930s, with bricks supplied by Ridgeons.

Above: The library today.

contractors had become rather more relaxed about accepting so many bricks all at once.

All this activity did not mean that business was easy. The slump, Cyril Ridgeon told his staff, was a time of 'grave anxiety. At times it has been difficult to find work for all'. Competition was fierce and a farthing (the smallest coin in circulation, worth a quarter of one old penny) either way per cubic foot of timber could win or lose an order. When every penny counted, Cyril insisted that envelopes from the daily mail should be slit open for use as writing paper and pencils should not be renewed until they had been sharpened down into nothing more than stubs. This lesson in thrift was one that his son also took to heart. Cyril told employees that the firm had succeeded through everyone working together and what gave him hope was his belief that 'so long as this spirit of cooperation continues we shall be able to stand four square to meet all competition from all corners'.

He made these remarks at a staff dinner held on 12 October 1931 at the Dorothy Café, a popular Cambridge venue, to celebrate Elliot's marriage that summer to Joan Miller, whose family ran the well-known music shop in Sidney Street, Cambridge. The appreciation of the contribution made to the firm by its employees was felt just as much by Elliot Ridgeon as by his father. One of the chief drawbacks of the existing bonus scheme was that it provided nothing for those who had retired and only paid out during times of profit. Cyril pointed out that it was Elliot who had persuaded him that it would be much more beneficial for staff if a pension fund was set up. It was Elliot who had been principally involved in finalising all the details in negotiation with the chosen insurance company.

In the same year the partnership was dissolved in favour of a limited company, Cyril Ridgeon & Son Ltd. Both incorporation and the pension fund gave greater security and more certainty for everyone involved in the business at a time when the slump was causing many firms to fail. By 1939 the company had enhanced this feeling of security by agreeing that every employee should be entitled to sickness benefit, a decision which prompted a petition of thanks from the staff.

The firm also made sure that annual outings continued throughout the depression and beyond. In 1930 the first outing made by coach went to the seaside at Clacton. In 1934 the company joined forces with several other local businesses, including Rattee & Kett, the stonemasons, and Heffer's Printing Works, to charter a special train from Cambridge to Brighton. En route the passengers passed close by the Crystal Palace, re-built at Sydenham, which would be destroyed by fire two years later. Ivor Warren described the pleasures of the day:

The myriad delights of Brighton provided entertainment for the whole day and all tastes were met by the various attractions; a few ventured to bathe from the shingle beach, others spent a lot of time on the two splendid piers, some riding on the Volks Electric Railway, others taking open-topped-deck buses up the Devil's Dyke, while some sat in the sun watching a giant diagrammatic scoreboard which recorded the minute by minute progress of the latest Test Match between England and Australia. It was without doubt the most eventful of the staff outings and a very contented party boarded the evening train from Brighton Central Station, reaching Cambridge round about midnight.

A similar outing followed to Portsmouth and Southsea in 1935, and staff also took the train to a much closer resort, Great Yarmouth, in 1936. The chartered train to Scarborough in 1937, shared once again with several other firms, left Cambridge at five in the morning, with the weary travellers returning at three o'clock the following morning. At least a refreshment car had been hired for the first time. When the last outing before the war took place in 1939, the train that took everyone to Margate was equipped with a full restaurant car serving a full breakfast. The train left Cambridge at 4.30am and breakfast was taken at 6am – the breakfast menu hoped everyone would be 'free to enjoy the ozone' once the train had pulled into Margate at 9am. For Peter Silk, who had joined the firm at the age of 14 in 1937, the day was almost ruined before it began. With two shillings in his pocket to last him all day, he lost the lot on the way down when he fell in with a group of older boys who were gambling. One of them, Josh Reed, told him he really should not have been gambling at his age and asked him how much he had lost. When Peter told him he had nothing left, Josh gave him a few shillings to see him through the day. It was another long day for the train journey home did not begin until 11.30pm, with coffee and sandwiches served on board. The exhausted revellers must have reached Cambridge around four in the morning, nearly 24 hours after they had set off.

Trips like these were some compensation for long hours of hard work. In the yards everything was still done by hand. Unloading a six-ton rail truck filled with slates or tiles took 12 man-hours to discharge, employing two men with handcarts capable of carrying at most two hundredweight. Wooden-framed, steel-banded packs of plywood or wallboard, each weighing between five and eight hundredweight, delivered in common user wagons, had to be lifted

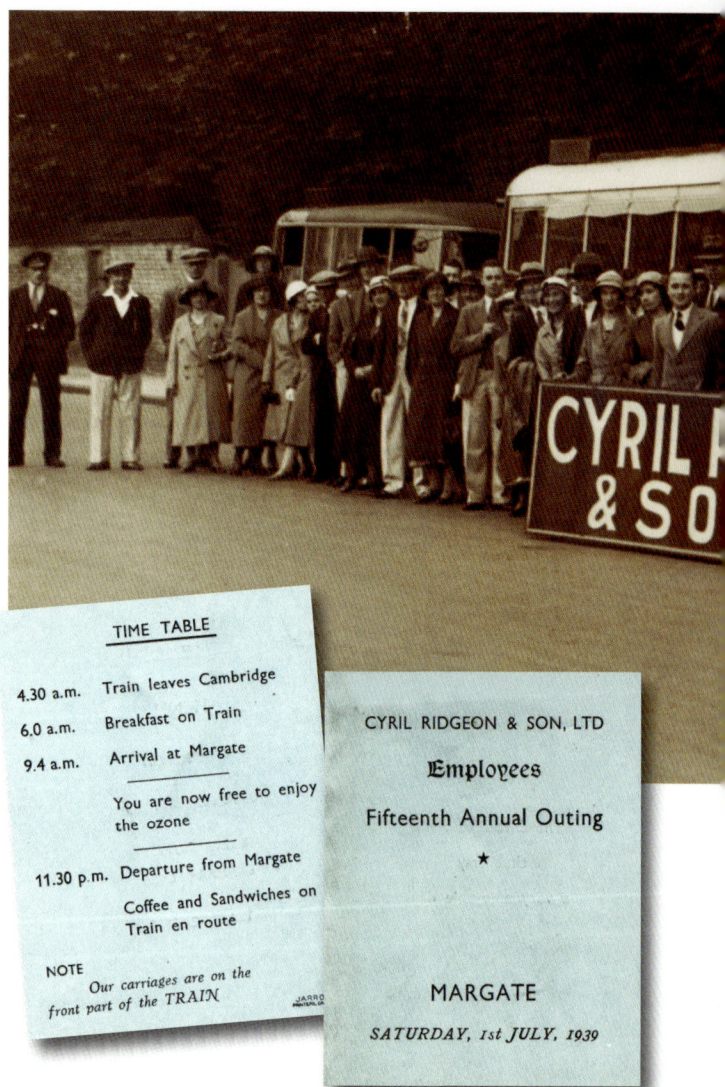

Above: Timetable for the outing to Margate, 1939.

This and facing page, clockwise from top: Staff trip to Felixstowe, 1933; Trip to Clacton, 1930; Josh Reed in the Tenison Road office.

over the truck side or pulled out through narrow door openings – as Ivor Warren noted, 'much leverage, sweat and bad language all combined to obtain a satisfactory discharge'. Timber too was manhandled piece by piece.

Mouldings and planed sizes of timber were kept in stock at Tenison Road, but most timber was located at Cavendish Road. The company was buying an extraordinary array of timber during the 1930s; the list included ash, birch, elm, poplar, western red cedar, hemlock, jarrah, African and Honduras mahogany, Baltic, American, Japanese, Austrian and English oak, parana, British Columbia, Siberian, yellow and pitch pine, silver spruce, sycamore, Iroko and Yang,

Burma and Moulmein teak, satin and American black walnut, and African (obechi) and American whitewood. The replacement of traditional products continued. Sawn laths gave way to plasterboard for ceilings and it was also used for partition walls. Slates were replaced by tiles, both those produced in the UK and those imported from Holland and Belgium, which were more easily available, thanks to the Harwich–Zeebrugge ferry.

Another innovation came in 1931 when 'light side' products (as opposed to 'heavy side', that is, building materials, bricks, blocks and pipes) were stocked for the first time, including paint and ironmongery, sanitaryware, and fittings for kitchens and bathrooms. Leslie Ridgeon also introduced independent tiled fire surrounds, then becoming fashionable, and displayed them in the window of Honeybunn's shop in recently redeveloped Hobson Street in the centre of Cambridge. Then in December 1932 the company opened a completely new branch at 44 Hobson Street. Here not only tiled fire surrounds were on display. The boom in private housing brought many families their first purpose-built bathroom, making bathroom suites a standard part of the fittings and fixtures. Leslie Ridgeon spotted another opportunity and stocked and displayed white baths and black and white stencilled tiles, later adding coloured suites in pastel shades as people became more affluent. Leslie Ridgeon found he had a flair for display, and the Hobson Street branch proved very successful. In 1937 one member of staff, Arthur Chapman, made up a tiled fire surround as a Union Jack in celebration of the Coronation that summer.

Inside the Hobson Street showroom.

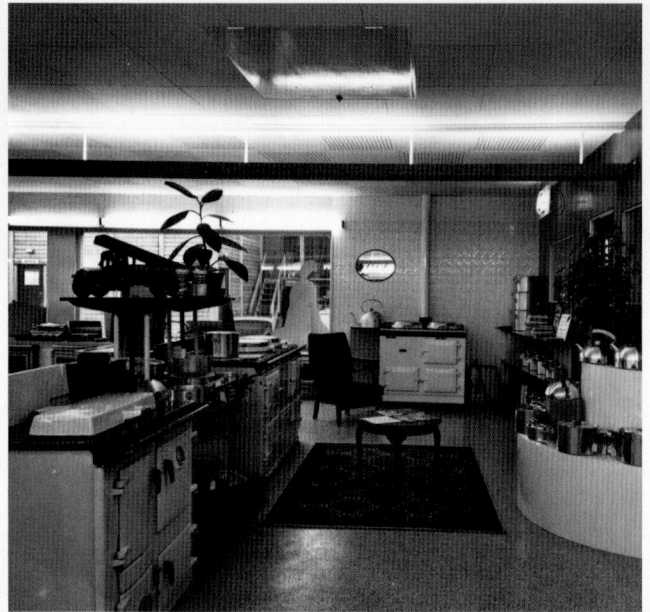

Number 44 Hobson Street. Staff rarely missed an opportunity to embellish the shopfront. Arthur Chapman made up a tiled fire surround as a Union Jack to celebrate the Coronation of King George VI in the summer of 1937, and pictured (above) in 1953, is the outside of the shop decorated with banners and Union Jack flags to mark the Coronation of Queen Elizabeth II.

The Hobson Street showroom was where Peter Silk started with the firm in 1937. He had wanted to stay at school but money was short at home so he had to go out to work. There were just three staff members: Alan Butler, the manager, Ron Kitson and Silk himself. As the junior, he earned ten shillings a week, working from quarter past eight in the morning until six o'clock in the evening, including Saturdays, with a half-day on a Thursday. Expected to keep the place clean and tidy, one of his duties included the weekly application of a mixture of milk and water to the two huge ferns in the entrance to make sure they looked bright and shiny. He also had to carry the daily takings up to John Rivers at Tenison Road, a responsibility it is difficult to contemplate being given to a lone youngster today. Most of the customers, he recollected, were fairly affluent. When the company acquired the sole rights to selling and servicing the renowned Aga cookers throughout East Anglia in the 1930s, this too was based at Hobson Street. Bringing in the major farming families among others, it was reckoned that the purchase of an Aga from the shop would encourage customers to buy all the other goods they needed as well.

Leslie Ridgeon seemed to be everywhere in the company during the 1930s. He assumed the role of general manager, and one of his responsibilities continued to be company transport. Lorries bearing the badges of Ford, Fordson and Chevrolet, Morris and Bedford joined the fleet. In 1932 the first articulated lorries, two Bedford-Eagles, were acquired.

Silver Jubilee celebration, Dorothy Café, 1936. Back row, from left: Mrs Gladys Ridgeon, Mr Leslie Ridgeon, Mrs Doris Rivers, Mr John Rivers, Mrs Cornell, Mr Bill Cornell, Mrs Law, Mr Law. The names of the couple first and second right are unknown. Front row: Mr Gordon Wellman, Mrs Joan Ridgeon, Mr Elliot Ridgeon, Mrs Kerridge, Mr Cyril Ridgeon, Mrs Beatrix Ridgeon, Mr Kerridge, Mrs Kidman and Mr Kidman.

The number of drivers grew as well, featuring men like Johnny Naylor, Howard Jarman, Percy Moule, Ernest Keys, Fred Bigmore and Ken Stone. Ken, the son of Joe Stone, was probably the first example in a long line of several members of the same family working for the company. By 1936 the company operated ten lorries. To give customers a better service, drivers would often be sent to bring back goods from all over the country.

New garages to house this growing fleet were added at Cavendish Road in 1936. There was a steady stream of other improvements, ranging from a new cross-cut saw, sprinkler system and dust extractor for the mill to the installation of a basic hot water system in the mess house and the construction, beginning in 1936, of three staff houses.

In December 1936 the company celebrated its 25th anniversary with another dinner at the Dorothy Café. It was attended by the company's 56 staff, their partners and customers, who enjoyed a menu of oxtail soup, fillets of sole with shrimp sauce, roast turkey and all the trimmings, Christmas pudding or trifle, cheese and biscuits and coffee. From 9pm, they were entertained with songs, sketches and monologues performed by the Magpies Concert Party. The event gave Cyril Ridgeon the chance to reflect on the reasons why the business had survived and prospered. He outlined clearly all those factors that have been an integral part of Ridgeons since its foundation, remarking:

If I were asked the cause of our steady increase, I think I should say it was good service – keeping good stocks and serving customers promptly with what they wanted, when they wanted it and how they wanted it, and giving a general feeling of confidence to those who dealt with us, so that they felt that our word is our bond, and when we say we will do anything, we will do it. Secondly, I feel that it is due to the hearty cooperation of our staff. I am sure I am right when I say that each one feels responsible for doing his or her best and would feel it keenly if, by any step, they let the Firm down.

Another equally important characteristic was outlined by one of the guests, Gordon Wellman, managing director of Rattee & Kett, a well-known local firm of builders and stonemasons. Responding to the toast, he noted that Ridgeons was regarded by the trade 'as a sort of builders' encyclopaedia, or Kelly's Directory'. He continued that 'it is very useful to have someone so near at hand who can tell us all about building materials that we don't know ourselves'.

By then Elliot Ridgeon had taken over day to day control of the whole business as his father's health continued to deteriorate. Cyril Ridgeon had managed to make a long-desired visit with other members of the Timber Trade Federation to North America in 1938, but the strenuous journey undermined his health. He formally relinquished his role as managing director in 1939. By then, under Elliot's guidance, the company was steadily expanding its sales territory. George Barber, for instance, was appointed as traveller for mid-Suffolk, including Bury St Edmunds and Sudbury. In 1939 all this had enabled the company's turnover to reach £115,000, worth about £5.3m today, based on changes in the RPI, earning profits of £6,000, the equivalent of nearly £280,000.

3

'The Governor'
1939–58

Above: 'The Governor', Elliot Ridgeon served as Mayor from 1956 to 1957. He is shown here in full regalia with his wife, Mayoress Joan, performing one of his many official duties.

BY 1939 THE COMPANY had supplied materials for a wide range of projects funded through the rearmament programme. These included the country's first radar station at Bawdsey in Suffolk and local aerodromes at Bassingbourn, Debden and Wyton. As the international situation became increasingly grave, the company was inundated with orders for materials for air raid shelters and blackout preparations. Partial conscription was introduced before war broke out, requiring young men aged 20 and 21 to carry out six months' military training, and at the end of August reservists began to be called up.

Previous pages: The new March branch, Cambridgeshire, which opened in January 1990. It was in 1948 that Ridgeons first expanded into the town of March by opening a shop in Broad Street.

This page: The declaration of war in 1939 saw many people offering their services as Civil Defence Volunteers. Several Ridgeons' employees followed Elliot's lead in joining the Air Raid Precautions (ARP) and becoming responsible for enforcing the blackouts. Sandbagging was employed throughout Cambridge (right) to protect buildings against bomb blasts. The Tenison Road office (below) was no exception.

To accommodate all these men, vast hutted camps were erected, and in and around Cambridgeshire contractors turned to Ridgeons for supplies of weatherboarding, matchings, battens, fillets and mouldings. The company had to introduce a second shift in the mill at Cavendish Road to cope with demand.

Among those leaving the company for military service before war was declared were Alan Butler and Ron Kitson, while Elliot Ridgeon, John Rivers and Ivor Warren all joined Air Raid Precautions (ARP). Warren later remembered the day war broke out. On Sunday, 3 September 1939 a small band of men had gathered at Tenison Road to fill and stack sandbags, intended to protect the offices against bomb blasts. 'Someone had brought along a radio set and whilst

the helpers worked they listened to the Prime Minister's sombre voice as he announced that Britain was, from 11am, in a state of war with Germany.'

The air raid warning sounded frequently in the first days after the war, all false alarms, but sufficient to send people scurrying to Ridgeons to stock up on building materials. Day after day counter staff were joined by office staff and salesmen to deal with the queues, working from 7.30am until 11pm, seven days a week. Ivor Warren described the scene: 'It became impossible to load vehicles for dispatch as the throngs crowded round using bicycles, handcarts, prams or any other form of conveyance to take away corrugated-iron sheets, bricks, cement, Sisalkraft and various sizes of timber'.

Learning the lessons of the previous conflict, the government quickly imposed strict controls over most materials once war was declared. House building ground to a halt. Private building works worth more than £500 had to be licensed by the newly created Ministry of Works & Buildings. The Controller of Building Materials now regulated the prices and supplies of almost all materials. Labour and materials were soon in short supply, and productivity in the industry declined sharply. Then there were fuel rationing and transport difficulties as the railways

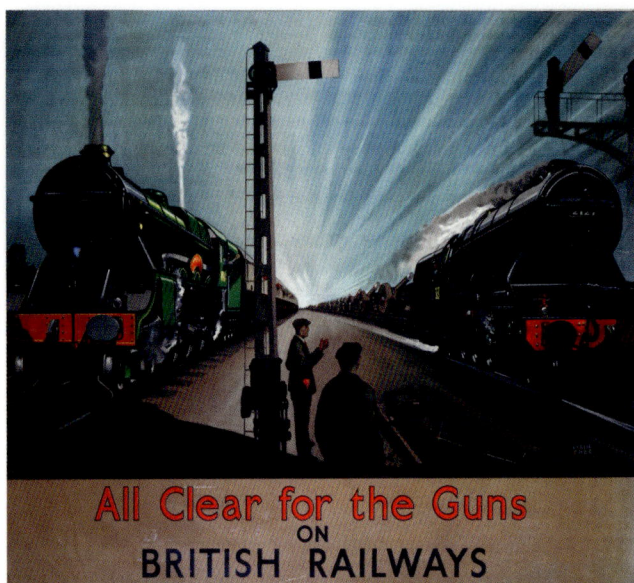

All Clear for the Guns ON BRITISH RAILWAYS

IS YOUR JOURNEY REALLY NECESSARY?

RAILWAY EXECUTIVE COMMITTEE

RAILWAY EQUIPMENT IS WAR EQUIPMENT

Guns, shells and bombs are not the only munitions of war

Above: Posters illustrating the wartime disruption to the railways.

Right: Four wartime Ridgeons employees (from right) Cyril Smith, Clifford Palmer, William 'Bill' Feakes and Ivor Warren.

damage by enemy action'. The Timber Control, the government agency in charge of timber, relied as it had in the First World War on working in partnership with experienced timber merchants. Stocks of soft wood, home grown timber and plywood were held not only at Tenison Road and Cavendish Road but also at Linton, Burwell and Toft in Cambridgeshire and Harlow in Essex. A gang of men under the direction of Harold Whitmore moved between them as necessary. A timber mill for home-grown timber was set up, with logs brought in from Forestry Commission woodland around Brandon and Thetford. The company was also responsible for emergency stocks held for the Ministry of War at several locations throughout the county, including Cambridge, Comberton and Offord, and at Saffron Walden in Essex. Supplies of timber from Russia and the Baltic dried up, replaced by more timber from North America.

Military supplies were necessarily a large part of the company's wartime business. The company was constantly busy with orders for the new aerodromes being built all over the county. Later, from the summer of 1942, the first American airmen began arriving, and more airfields were constructed. Among the RAF stations supplied by Ridgeons were those at Oakington, Waterbeach, Fowlmere, Bottisham, Witchford, Bourn, Tempsford and Warboys; while US air bases included Molesworth, Grafton Underwood, Polebrook, Chelveston, Kimbolton, Lakenheath, Honington,

became congested and unpredictable. For many merchants, the burdens were too heavy and they went out of business, while others survived by supplying materials for civil defence and war damage work.

Ridgeons was more fortunate. The company's real strength during the war was the timber business. The Office of Works had written to the company in June 1939 asking if it would store timber on behalf of the government during any emergency. As Elliot Ridgeon later recorded, 'a number of merchants, like ourselves, situated strategically throughout the country, were made stockists of government supplies and materials for use in emergency after major

Above: Staff cutting logs during the war at the sawmill at Cavendish Road, c.1944. Timber was in short supply during the war and there were no imports. The little timber that was available was all home grown. From left, unknown, Ernest Maxim and Fred Ashberry.

Below: Mr Graham, a mechanic for Ridgeons during the war years, with one of the lorries from the Ridgeons fleet, a Bedford 'three-tonner', outside the gates of Westminster College.

Stansted and Bexwell. The link with the US military continued after the war and would eventually extend to US bases on the Continent as well as in the UK.

The British and American military often picked up the timber they required direct from the yards. On one occasion a convoy of a dozen army trucks arrived with instructions to collect twelve loads of timber; in fact, the order was for just twelve pieces. To save face, the lieutenant in charge had his corporals load one piece of timber onto each truck.

Towards the end of the war all this work on the airfields encouraged Bill Feakes, who had joined as an office boy in 1930, to start up a plant hire section. Large Benford cement mixers, compressors and paint sprays were hired out to contractors laying down runways and aprons on the airfields. It was heavy work loading such machinery onto ordinary lorries, but only towards the end of the war was it possible to acquire a Scammell low-loader trailer with a winch.

The company's own trucks worked hard during the war. Three trucks were requisitioned by the authorities, but – under special arrangements – they were replaced by two more Bedfords. These covered thousands and thousands of miles during the war, collecting and delivering bricks,

timber and repair materials to airfields, army bases and defence units. Often travelling in near darkness under blackout conditions, the company's drivers, including Len Bigmore, Ken Stone, Victor Keys and Bill Batterbee, had to contend with speed limits of 20 or 30 miles an hour (not that the trucks could have travelled much faster). The removal of signposts, intended to bamboozle any invader, made collections from locations in other parts of the country, from Billingham and Birkenhead to Hereford, Emsworth and Lowestoft, a somewhat fraught experience. Precious but essential assets, these trucks were often commandeered by the local Home Guard at the weekends. The company's drivers, although they were not compelled to take part in these exercises, always went along for fear of leaving their lorries in less experienced hands.

Civil defence work became more and more important. After the London Blitz began in the autumn of 1940, the scale of the damage led to requests for emergency stockists

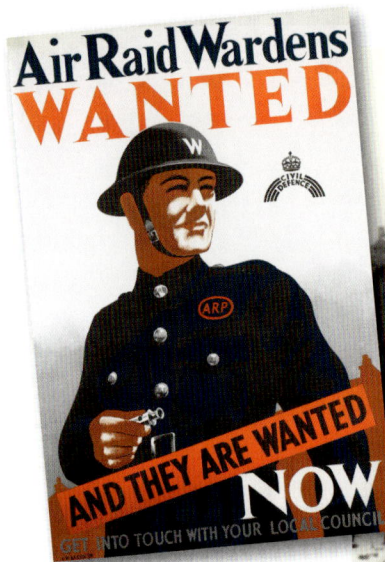

Above: ARP recruitment poster.

Right: Nine people were killed when bombs fell on several homes in Vicarage Street in June 1940.

outside the capital, Ridgeons among them, to supply building materials. Elliot Ridgeon and Harold Whitmore were besieged with telephone calls at all hours of the day and night from officials calling for the firm's assistance. The company carried a stock ranging from tarpaulins, tiles and slates, chimney pots and roofing materials, to glazing materials, bricks, cement and plaster. After a full day at work, drivers such as Howard Jarman, Johnny Naylor and Percy Moule would load up their lorries and drive into London, sometimes in the middle of an air raid. This work carried on throughout the war, particularly towards the end, when the capital came under the onslaught of the V1 flying bombs and the V2 rockets. These errands became known within the company as 'Flying Bomb Specials'. 'The first of these,' Elliot Ridgeon later recalled, 'was, I believe, something of a convoy when Messrs Bigmore, Jarman and Naylor made an all-night trip to London following a normal day's work to take tarpaulins to cover the roofs of houses unfortunate enough to be affected by the blast of Doodle Bugs.'

Cambridge did not escape the air raids. Those initial false alarms bred some complacency, so there was considerable shock when the first attack did occur on the evening of 18–19 June 1940. A number of bombs intended for the railway fell instead on Vicarage Street, off Sturton Street, in Cambridge, killing nine people, one of them an evacuee

from London. One of the company's customers, Len Palmer, had gone up the road prior to the raid to talk to friends. He came back to find his home destroyed and his family dead. Ivor Warren remembered that 'the next morning Mr Howlett of Bryant & Howlett, Abbey Walk, wheeled his handcart into Tenison Road to collect coffin boards for the victims. His face registered the horror of the night's happenings.' Raids in and around the town occurred sporadically during the rest of the war. The closest the company came to harm was on 20 January 1941 when a single bomber worked its way down the railway from Coldham's Lane Station. Fortunately, the last of its bombs had been dropped before the plane reached Tenison Road.

Elliot Ridgeon was the senior ARP warden for Trumpington and part of South Cambridge and John Rivers for Coleridge Road, while Ivor Warren was a deputy senior warden in Perne Road. Leslie Ridgeon and Bill Cornell helped to form the Local Defence Volunteers, later the Home Guard, in Cherry Hinton. Elliot took his turn fire watching at Tenison Road along with other senior male staff. This usually lasted from eight in the evening until seven in the morning. At Cavendish Road, where Bill Cornell acted as caretaker during the war, new offices were built and the old ones used for fire watching. At Tenison Road a shelter was constructed in front of the offices. In the event of a raid, staff members were instructed on the sound of the sirens to

Above: To cope with the inevitable staff shortages brought on by the war, many extra hands, both male and female – some of whom were relatives of employees called up for service – were drafted in to assist in the smooth running of the business. Front row: Miss Cornell, Miss Francis, Miss Wosencroft, Miss Squires, Miss Pearson, Miss Elliot (later Mrs Nunn) and Miss Jacobs, a wartime refugee. Pictured (centre) is Mr Jackson, a long-time friend of Cyril, who helped out in the office.

Below right: List of Ridgeons staff called up for the war. Thankfully, all Ridgeons employees returned home alive.

letter or newsletter a postal order for five shillings for 'smokes' or anything else he could buy.

The company generally coped with the shortage of labour in the same way as many other businesses, calling former employees out of retirement and employing older men or those rejected as unfit for military service. Among the exceptions was Jimmy Nunn, who joined as an office boy in June 1940, earning 15 shillings a week until he too was later called up. He had studied architecture at Cambridgeshire Technical College, but with no building going on he joined Ridgeons instead. Just next to the yard at Tenison Road was the coal chute, built in the 1930s, which tipped up trucks of coal into tenders for the steam locomotives; Nunn remembered how it cast 'a dark mist over the place'. The office, he found out, was full of high desks and tall stools with huge, thick ledgers 'as heavy as lead', all locked away every night. Quite a number of the office staff were youngsters, under 18, 'full of verve and vigour', running rings around John Rivers. With so little office work to do in the early days of the war, the boys were often sent out on errands on their bicycles, and they frequently ended up in the café in East Road.

During the latter part of the war a small number of Italian prisoners of war, ferried back and forth from the camp at

evacuate the office, but only after placing cash, books and papers in the safes. Jimmy Nunn remembered how he would be sent up on to the roof during the day, ready to signal the approach of enemy aircraft by stamping his foot repeatedly. Elliot and Leslie Ridgeon usually remained in or close by the offices. Like the rest of his staff, Elliot Ridgeon never took a day's holiday during the war. His own duties were increased when he also took on the post of Controller of Machine Tool Allocation for East Anglia. Bank holidays were often cancelled and the demands of wartime meant that staff frequently worked seven days a week. By the end of the war the working week had become standardised, running from 7.30 a.m. to 6 p.m. between Monday and Friday. Most staff worked on Saturday mornings and key personnel on Sundays, although usually on a rota and only for the morning.

Labour became increasingly scarce. From Ridgeons, 33 men, representing more than half the company's staff at the outbreak of war, were eventually called up. The company began sending them regular letters, keeping them up to date with news of the business. Eventually the letters were replaced with a newsletter, edited by John Rivers, which carried on after the war, lasting until 1967. The newsletter also carried messages sent in return from those in service at home or overseas. Each month every man received with his

CYRIL RIDGEON & SON LIMITED
CAMBRIDGE

The following members of our Staff are serving with the Forces.

NAME	SERVICE	RANK	REMARKS
ANDREWS, G.	R.A.F.	AC2	
BARBER, R.A.L.	Dental Corps	Corporal	
BARBER, G.	Royal Engineers	Corporal	
BATTERBEE, W.	R.A.F.	AC1	
BENMENT, C.	R.A.S.C.	Driver	
BURNS, R.	R.E., Cambs.Regt.	Private	Discharged
BUTLER, A.R.	R.A.F.	Sergt. Observer	Prisoner of War (Germany) Repatriated
COULSON, A.	R.A.F.	AC1	
GEORGE, A.J.	Suffolk Regt.	Private	
HARRISON, F.	R.A.F.	LAC	
KITSON, R.	1st. Batt. Cambs.	Sergeant	Missing (Singapore)
LEE, A.	Cambs. Regt.	Private	
REED, R.	R.A.F.	LAC	
WILLIAMS, D.	R.A.F.	AC2	
SILK, P.	R.N.	Ord. Seaman	
LEEKE, L.O.	R.A.S.C.	Driver	
CORNELL, R.J.	R.C.S.	Sgmn.	
CHALKLEY, K.	R.N.	Ord. Seaman	
NUNN, R.J.	R.A.C.	Trooper	
TANNER, S	Royal Engineers	Driver	
VICKERS, C.	Royal Marines	Marine	Discharged
DEAN, F.	R.N.	P.S.A.	
KATZ, R.	R.E.M.E.	Craftsman	
GRAY, N.	Pioneer Corps	Private	

"It is the evil things we fight against — brute force, bad faith, injustice, oppression".
PRIME MINISTER, HON. NEVILLE CHAMBERLAIN
3RD. SEPT. 1939

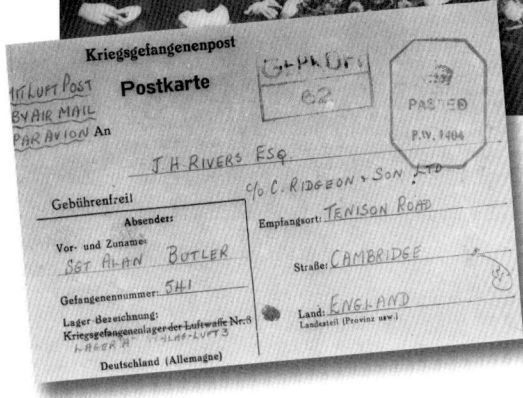

Top: Staff gather to celebrate the returning prisoners of war, including Ron Kitson.

Above: Postcard from Alan Butler, an observer in the Flying Corps, to the firm. Sergeant Butler's plane was shot down, and he became a prisoner of war. The postcard was reassuring news to Mr Ridgeon that Butler was still alive.

Facing page: The American Cemetery stands in Cambridge as the only British memorial to the fallen American soldiers of the Second World War. Ridgeons supplied timber and materials to both the British and American military during the war, and US soldiers would often collect their orders from the yards.

Trumpington, helped out in the Cavendish Road yard. They showed an understandable reluctance to work, several losing themselves for as long as possible in the yard, and they made the most of the language barrier, but in general they worked happily enough alongside the rest of the staff.

Cyril Ridgeon never lived to see the return of peace. He died at home in Cambridge at the age of 68 in January 1942 after a long and painful illness. His son would later recall how he had become 'a frail little figure'. Joan Pearson, one of the office girls, probably reflected the feelings of most of those who knew him when, many years later, she summed up Cyril Ridgeon as 'a very kind gentleman, who, I think, looked on the staff almost as an extension of his family'.

Military activity in and around the town increased as preparations were made for the invasion of Europe. Now the skies above Cambridge were filled with sound of Allied planes heading for the Continent. One spring morning in 1944 workers at Tenison Road discovered US sentries posted on the gate, demanding proof of identity before allowing them through. Later General Eisenhower, the American commander-in-chief, emerged from a special train with sleeping cars attached that had been resting in the siding. He was on his way, as it turned out, to a conference about plans for D-Day. Two weeks later a similar train stopped in the siding, this time containing General Montgomery, the British commander, who stood up as he was driven away in an open car and waved at cheering staff grouped outside the office.

Cyril Ridgeon & Son Ltd more than held its own during the war. While turnover, which reached £156,000 in 1945, was little more in real terms than in 1939, the company's profits rose to £23,000, the equivalent of nearly £740,000 today, a substantial increase. Moreover, the business had almost doubled its workforce, from 59 to 100, leading to suggestions that sports teams could be formed and the company could join the Cambridge Business Houses Sports Club. Connections had been made with the large construction firms involved in military projects in the area, mainly thanks to Cyril Briant, who continued as a representative after the war, and the boundaries of the company's sales territory had been widened further (in 1944, for instance, a salesman had been appointed for Peterborough & District).

After the war 27 staff members returned to the company, the remaining six having found alternative employment. Not all of them returned immediately to the firm. Ron Kitson and Alan Butler each required a long spell of convalescence, having spent most of the war as prisoners. Kitson had served as a sergeant major in the Cambridgeshire Regiment in Singapore, and just before it fell to the Japanese he hid the regimental drums. He endured the horrors of a Japanese camp after being captured but returned to Singapore to discover the drums exactly where they had been hidden. Alan Butler had been held in Germany after being shot down over Libya in 1941. When Kitson made his first visit to the company after returning home in the autumn of 1945, the newsletter recorded how 'he has grown from a boy to man and certainly looks big and strong although we are informed he is on a milk and egg diet plus vitamin tablets'. Kitson convalesced at the county hospital, where he had a visit from Peter Silk, who had come back from service at sea. The newsletter, which noted how Silk was 'taller than ever', remarked that 'you can imagine the welcome they gave

each other after so long a time'. Kitson eventually started work again at Hobson Street in the spring of 1946. Silk had earlier written to the editor in February 1945 how, on his way back from naval service, he had been able to eat bananas; it was a year later before the newsletter could record how 'we have seen bananas in the shops and some of us have been fortunate to taste them again'. All those servicemen who came back from the war benefited from a small homecoming fund the company had set up. On 5 December 1946 they received a formal welcome at a special dinner held at the University Arms Hotel. Cyril Ridgeon's widow, Beatrice, as chairman of the company, made the presentations. In return, the returnees presented Elliot Ridgeon with a set of gold cufflinks.

With the imposition of economic austerity in peacetime as a consequence of the crippling burden of paying for the war, many wartime controls were retained and new ones introduced. All repairs and maintenance were regulated until 1948, and controls over new building work were not

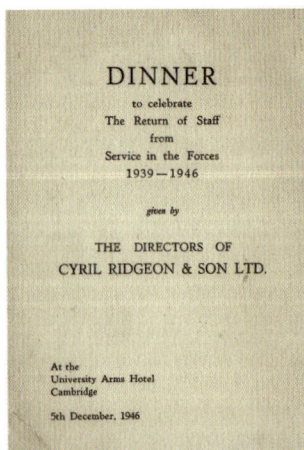

THE DIRECTORS OF CYRIL RIDGEON & SON LTD.
request the pleasure of the company of

at a DINNER to be held at
The University Arms Hotel (Park Terrace Entrance)
on Thursday, 5th December, 1946
7 p.m. for 7.30 p.m.

R.S.V.P.
to Mr. J. H. Rivers
by 22nd November.

DINNER
to celebrate
The Return of Staff
from
Service in the Forces
1939—1946

given by

THE DIRECTORS OF
CYRIL RIDGEON & SON LTD.

At the
University Arms Hotel
Cambridge

5th December, 1946

Menu
—
Clear Vermicelli or Thick Pea Soup
—
Roast Stuffed Turkey and Sausages
Brussels Sprouts
Roast Potatoes
—
Sultana Pudding
or
Rum and Coffee Ice Cream
—
Coffee
—
Draught Beer
Cider or Fruit Drinks

Top: Employees who returned from the war gathered for a celebration dinner in 1946.

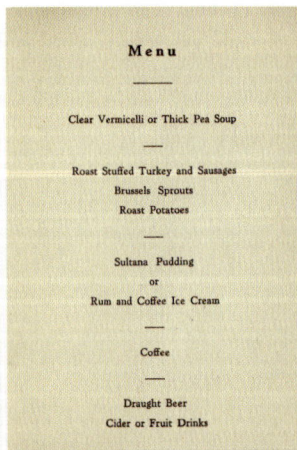

Above: The evening's dinner menu.

Top right: Peter Silk's invitation.

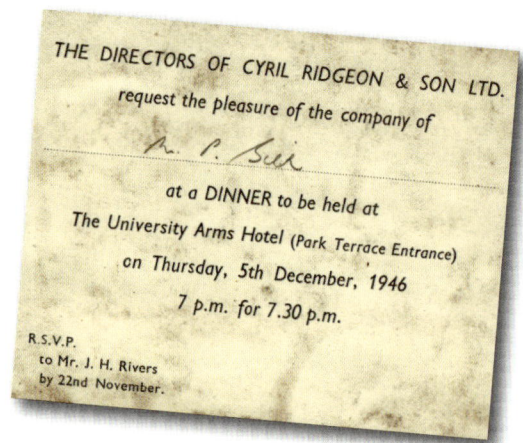

removed until 1955. At Ridgeons two men were employed full time in administering the necessary rules and regulations. The government's priorities lay in repairing war damage, providing public housing and building new schools. The shortage of skilled labour and materials persisted, stimulating the use of alternatives and the widespread adoption of innovative construction techniques. While timber and steel, which were still rationed, as well as bricks, which were not, remained scarce, so too were items such as plasterboard. There were also lengthy delays in fulfilling orders for new plant, since most of it was sold abroad to bring in valuable foreign currency. In the late 1940s the waiting time for a new cement mixer was ten months. In November 1946 *Ridgeon News* listed long delivery periods for vices, saws, chisels and planes, while supplies of hammers, hacksaws, blowlamps, spanners, bradawls, files, rules, tapes, hand drills and hatchets were limited. The lack of skilled labour led firms to adopt heavy plant and light equipment, such as tubular scaffolding and power tools. Prefabrication and concrete helped to overcome the shortage of bricks and other materials. It was only after 1955, once prosperity had returned and the final controls had been removed, that private housing, for instance, once again became profitable.

After the war the company continued to make progress, whether in times of shortage or in times of plenty. Its reputation for fairness, displayed under wartime conditions, as well as the good working relationship the business enjoyed with both officialdom and customers, held it in good stead when controls were retained after the war. Elliot Ridgeon was very clear about the criteria for success. In notes he prepared in 1952 for a talk on the builders' merchant, it was service that he emphasised most strongly. The merchant must offer his customers extensive stock, prompt delivery

and wide knowledge. In the postwar era these three factors would become synonymous with Ridgeons. Elliot noted how 'to the busy builder, the merchant's representative is a real friend'. Elliot Ridgeon also believed it was important for builders to have the opportunity to see products on display. While he was clear that the merchant's priority must always be the builder, Elliot was also keenly aware of the importance of offering equally high standards of service to members of the public. For one thing, this often stimulated orders for builders. He pointed out how something as simple as the cookery demonstrations, arranged by Mona Andrews and given regularly in the company's Hobson Street showrooms, not only stimulated the purchase of Aga cookers but acted as an incentive for customers to return after their cooker had been installed.

In early 1945 Ridgeons showed its commitment to keeping the trade knowledge of staff up to date by enrolling a number of them for lectures at the local technical college. One of those involved with the course was the company's mill manager, Ernest Maxim, who sadly died suddenly in April that year. Employees also attended a course at Hobson Street given by staff from the paint manufacturer, Sir W.A. Rose. In the autumn of the same year lectures on the building trade were organised at the University Arms Hotel and Miller's Music Studios in Sidney Street.

In 1946 it was possible to carry out some improvements at Tenison Road. The offices were extended and, more importantly, a new display area was created and the first purpose-built paint store was completed, under the management of Glyn Richards. More significant was the acquisition in July 1946 of the first branch of the business. Ridgeons

took over the long-established but old-fashioned hardware and ironmongery firm of Pilgrim & Son at 22 Broad Street, in March, the Fenland market town 20 miles north of Cambridge. In a part of the country still lacking mains electricity, the shop still sold a lot of paraffin and oil lamps. The manager, Mr Fowler, was recruited, and Leslie Ridgeon supervised the reconstruction and refurbishment of the building, which was supplied regularly with goods from Cambridge. Mr Stimpson, a heating engineer, was kept on, and several major heating jobs were carried out. The landscape could seem terribly bleak, and Elliot Ridgeon's younger son, Michael, who was just 11 at the time, later recalled his trepidation at accompanying his father into these wide-open spaces. 'My fear became almost unbearable when my father told me that we would probably be meeting some of the "fenland tigers" [a term associated with those who had been born in the Fens].'

Top: Daybreak over Fenland.   Above: 22 Broad Street, March.

Travel between Cambridge and March was not easy in those days for the area was susceptible to flooding. Communications were completely cut off during the winter of 1947, one of the worst on record in the UK. The big freeze began in late January 1947 and ceased only in mid-April, when the thaw, accompanied by strong winds, brought more flooding. Elliot Ridgeon remarked in February that 'since Christmas we have experienced as protracted a spell of bad weather conditions as most of us can remember'. It was so bitterly cold during the winter that staff in the March branch desperately tried to keep their hands warm over an upturned flowerpot heated by a candle underneath. The building trade completely shut down, and the inability to ship sufficient coal to the power stations led to the introduction of power cuts, which effectively closed the factories of many of the company's suppliers. Elliot recalled:

The situation then certainly looked pretty grim, and the possibility of 'short time' for the staff was clearly a probability. It has always been the endeavour of the Directors of this Company to ensure that everyone has a full week's pay packet, and we were in an extremely fortunate position in having sufficient orders to keep running to the end of February. It was fortunate that the Sawmill power is provided by Diesel Oil, otherwise we should, in common with other firms, have been forced to close down.

Once the winter was over, the new branch, under the supervision of Leslie Ridgeon, proved very successful. In 1948 a former builder's yard in Creek Road was leased, and the heating and engineering department from Broad Street was transferred there a year later. Despite this progress, it would be ten years before another acquisition was made, and even then the business concerned would be run separately from the rest of Ridgeons.

Leslie Ridgeon's flair for display was put to good use when the company began exhibiting at county agricultural shows. The first postwar Cambridgeshire Show, held in Wimpole Park on a brilliant summer's day in 1947, proved a huge success for the firm, which won the prize for best trade stand. For several years the company attended a number of agricultural shows, including those for Essex,

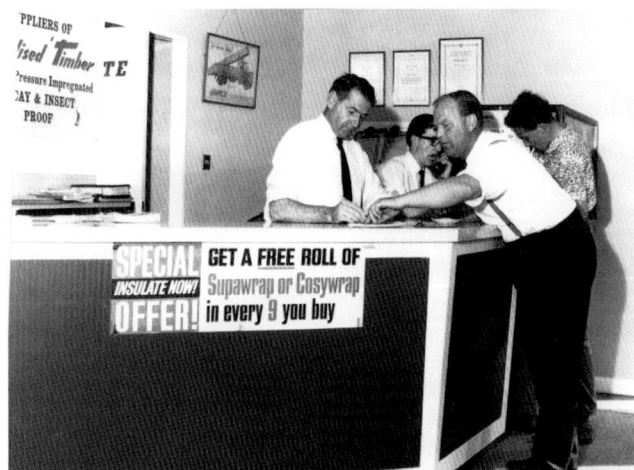

Above: Inside the Creek Road office. Behind the counter (foreground) is Ray Cornell (son of Bill) who is going over an order with Ron Abbs.

Left: Exterior of the new premises in Creek Road, March. A Ridgeons lorry leaves with a consignment of materials for its customers.

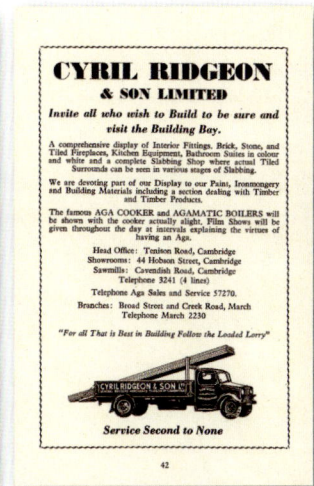

Suffolk and Huntingdonshire, as well as a trade show held on Midsummer Common in Cambridge, today the preserve of fairs and circuses as well as grazing cattle. With agriculture enjoying a renaissance, they proved particularly effective at increasing sales of Aga cookers. Leslie Ridgeon would have an Aga lit and under fire, ready for cookery demonstrations during the day. To every housewife buying an Aga, he would offer to come along to their home when it was fired up and demonstrate how to cook roast beef and Yorkshire puddings. Since the cookers were temperamental beasts, responsive to tender care, his offer was often accepted. The trade stands came to an end in the early 1960s as individual county shows gave way to regional shows, such as the East of England, where Ridgeons would not reappear until the late 1990s.

The company continued to press ahead with efforts to improve the trade knowledge of its workforce. In the summer of 1947 the newsletter, in pointing out how 'the Directors like to encourage members of the staff to improve their knowledge', announced that the company would contribute towards the cost of the fees for evening classes at the Cambridgeshire Technical College for both junior and more experienced staff. By 1949 the company was paying full fees for apprentices and half fees for everyone else.

As a young apprentice, Ray Langford's experience was typical. He joined the company from school at the age of 14

Ridgeons participated in a number of trade shows after the war, showcasing their wide range of equipment, materials and supplies. Their well-laid-out and innovative stands, which included cookery demonstrations on fully functioning Aga cookers, won them many prizes.

Clockwise from top left: Staff at trade show, 1950s; Selection of prize and commendation certificates won by Ridgeons in the 1940s and 1950s; Advertisement and programme for the Cambridge Trade Fair, 1953; Percy Moule and Roy Parkinson next to the installed Aga inside the show tent; The Ridgeons stand at the Norfolk show. The Ridgeons display frontage, made by Claxton was erected at each show and made an inviting spectacle for visitors.

in August 1944. After six months spent settling in, he began his formal indentured apprenticeship as a mechanic. This lasted for five years, followed by a further two as an improver, after which he became eligible for the top wage rate. He had two mentors but the first was sacked for smoking, a serious offence in the yard where so much material was combustible, and he learned most from his second mentor, Ted Aplin. Ray would eventually take over responsibility for the garage at Cavendish Road from Ted in 1955 and remained in charge until it was closed in 1987.

As well as staff, Ridgeons also included customers in its constant campaign for the improvement of trade knowledge – in 1953, for instance, a series of film lectures for customers and senior staff was arranged on topics such as 'Slating and Tiling', 'Lead in Building' and 'Bricks – How They Are Made and Used'.

Further improvements were made at the company's sites in Cambridge. In 1949 an ironmongery department was added at Tenison Road under Howard Jarman, and Clifford Palmer, while organising the weekly LBC allocation, expanded the brick department, devising a library to help customers choose specific bricks. At Cavendish Road a Dutch barn was erected for more storage and a new workshop was built. Timber still came into Cavendish Road by rail, the trucks shunted overnight into the siding, which was extended in 1949. Even in the late 1950s it was still being unloaded piece by piece by hand. Joinery timber was stored under cover, carried by men wearing shoulder-pads along walkways that ran straight into the sheds from the trucks. Timber for building was stored in the open, sorted

Programme for the series of film lectures arranged by Ridgeons for customers and senior staff. Topics covered included 'Slating and Tiling', 'Lead in Building' and 'Bricks – How They Are Made and Used', and the lectures ran from November 1953 to April 1954.

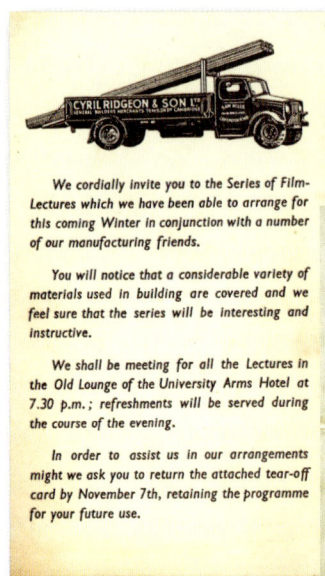

Ironmongery department at Tenison Road.

onto trailers towed around the yard before once more being unloaded by hand and stacked. Gradually more timber began to arrive from London docks on the firm's own articulated lorries, which were really too big to come down Cavendish Road. They often had difficulty getting beneath the Ridgeons sign above the gate and frequently took down the awning of the nearby boot repair shop. The owner, before he wound out the awning, got into the habit of asking whether or not the yard was receiving any timber deliveries that day.

Softwood was finally freed from licensing in 1953. Prior to this the rules had been relaxed to permit individuals to buy timber, up to the value of one pound, without requiring a licence. The intention of this concession was easily breached: individuals persuaded their friends to part with their entitlement to make a single worthwhile purchase.

Tenison Road still stocked some timber. When licensing was still in force, hardboard and insulation board came from Sweden in crates made of deal. John Doggett, who joined the company in 1950, remembered how the wooden crates were dismantled, the nails removed and the timber boards sold to a waiting list of customers. In the early 1950s half the goods received at Tenison Road still came by rail and, just like timber, everything had to be manhandled. The complaints to British Rail about damaged goods were so frequent that, John Doggett remembered, 'the British Rail claims man almost became a member of staff'. Theft on the railways was a serious problem – at least one wagon expected at Tenison Road never turned up and losses on bulk timber traffic to Cavendish Road compelled the company to transfer most of this business from rail to road.

The railways were only too aware of the growing threat from road transport and, during negotiations over the renewal of the lease for Tenison Road in 1953, British Rail attempted to insert a clause compelling the company to accept delivery of goods only by rail. Understandably, the company took exception to this, writing incredulously that 'surely you must realise that for some years now we have not been in a position to dictate whether goods travel by

Top left: Timber stacks at Cavendish Road, c.1950.

Left: Cavendish Road sawmill.

Top: Workmen hauling a large stack of treated timber from the Tanalith tank.

Above, left and right: Tanalith vacuum and pressure timber preservative impregnation plant.

road or rail'. British Rail dragged its feet over the negotiations. Renewal was due on 1 January 1954 and by March the company was writing: 'we think that the Railway Executive is treating us very hardly indeed. You must be fully aware that the insecurity of tenure is most disconcerting.' The company regarded the railway's proposal to grant a yearly tenancy as good as notice to quit. Even when the railway agreed to consider a longer lease, little happened. The file correspondence ends in August 1954 without a new lease being signed. A copy of the next lease shows that one was eventually signed, for a period of 21 years, in 1962.

In 1947 the company already operated 18 lorries. A number of three-wheeled tractors was acquired because their short turning circle proved ideal for town deliveries. They were all maintained from the garage in Cavendish Road, where Ron Coleman joined Ray Langford in 1955. A new motor workshop was also built at Cavendish Road in 1949. The transport manager for many years was Ivor Warren. Like so many other businesses, a lot of the vehicles acquired by the company during the 1950s were second-hand, often former military lorries. An exception was the new van bought in 1954 for the company's Red Arrow Service, which offered special deliveries for customers.

Throughout this period Elliot Ridgeon was firmly in charge. His moniker was 'the Governor' – he generally addressed staff by their surnames, and he was only ever called 'Mr Elliot' or 'Sir'. For some employees, he was a distant figure held in awe, and his straightforward manner was not calculated to put people at ease. His secretary in the early 1950s, Vima Linney, described Elliot as 'abrupt but very charming'. (One of his later secretaries was Betty Denny, the daughter of Bill Cornell, the first employee, who resigned following her marriage. She was followed by Molly Lawrence and Winifred Lumby, who on the death of Elliot continued with David until her retirement.) Elliot was also, recalled Terry Belcher, who joined the company at Cavendish Road in 1953, 'a stickler'. He walked around the yard every morning, checking everything. He rarely went on holiday, usually taking just a week at Hunstanton on the Norfolk coast, but always calling every manager each day to find out what was going on. Generally he expected to be consulted over every decision that was made, an approach that had an inadvertent impact on his managers. Many years later, towards the end of Elliot's life, one manager taking a call from a customer abruptly ended the conversation when he realised Elliot was calling him from the light flashing on his phone. Elliot would have been mortified to know that he was being given priority over a customer.

His key lieutenants were Leslie Ridgeon, John Rivers and Bill Feakes. They all held the title of executive director by the mid-1950s, although they did not sit on the board, where the directors consisted of Elliot Ridgeon, his wife Joan and his mother Beatrice.

Methodical and orderly, Elliot opened the post every morning, stamped every letter that went out of the office, reviewed and initialled every invoice, priced many enquiries, assisted by Peter Clark, followed by Neville Bacon, and expected to be told every day exactly how much money had been paid out, ensuring that the overdraft was never exceeded. He had come through the depression and the habit of counting every penny never left him, which sometimes prevented him from spending money when it was necessary. He had grown up when it was usual for staff themselves to make requests for pay increases rather than have them awarded automatically, and this too was a habit he found difficult to break.

But he also inherited from his father an innate sense of fairness, particularly towards those who worked for him, and was deeply interested in their welfare, as was his wife, Joan. He introduced long-service awards in 1946, with 'meritorious' service of more than five years being rewarded with additional days of paid holiday. The scheme

Clockwise from top left: Elliot Ridgeon and his 'key lieutenants', Leslie Ridgeon, John Rivers and Bill Feakes.

Left: Delivery fleet and staff, 1956. Key staff members shown include Ray Rush (first left), Percy Moule (third left), Tony Mathews (fourth left), 'Smoky' Crane, Bob Hunter, Ken Stone (sixth, seventh and eighth from left), Ken Bowyer, Harry Carter (eleventh and thirteenth from left). Sid Stone is shown far right.

maintained the then common distinction between white-collar and blue-collar workers, with office staff eligible for a maximum of one week's additional holiday after 25 years, while yard, mill and other workers were limited to three days after 30 years. Those with 25 or more years of service received a gold watch; one recipient in 1952 was Ken Stone, whose father Joe and uncle Sid had already completed their 25 years. Staff called up for national service still received their monthly five shillings postal order. All those with more than a year's service were entitled to an annual bonus. Staff were given vouchers at Christmas, and for several years the directors paid for children of staff to attend the pantomime at the New Theatre in Cambridge. Eligibility for the voluntary contributory pension scheme was reduced from five years' service to three in 1949. To celebrate 40 years in business in 1951, it was agreed that work should end half an hour earlier on Saturdays. Holidays were standardised for all staff in 1953, with everyone receiving two weeks' paid holiday after one year's service, in addition to public holidays. In the same year private health insurance was offered to staff for the first time.

Elliot revived the pre-war tradition of annual outings. The first one took place in June 1947 when four coaches took staff to London for the day. In 1948 the responsibility for planning this trip every year was transferred to the newly formed social club, under the chairmanship of Bill Feakes. London was a popular destination, and no outing was complete without a visit to one show or another. In 1949 staff chose between Oklahoma, Annie, Get Your Gun, the Crazy Gang and the Marx Brothers. There were trips to the seaside, including Clacton, Margate, Southend and Great Yarmouth. On the outing to Margate in 1957 more than 200 people took part. The distinction between white-collar and blue-collar workers was acute – after the coaches had stopped at a pub on the way back, John Rivers asked Jimmy Nunn accusingly, 'You didn't go into the bar with the men, did you?' Through the social club, sports teams were formed as the workforce expanded, from football and cricket to darts and table tennis.

Elliot Ridgeon's ability to retain daily control of an increasingly diverse business, with well over 150 staff by the late 1950s, owed much to his phlegmatic approach to business. He was, recalled David Ridgeon, a 'fairly easy' man, although his son felt he never had a particularly clear view of the long-term development of the business. Elliot knew from experience that there would be bad times as well as good. When his younger son, Michael, wondered how he could remain so calm under pressure, he replied: 'Michael, you only get overwrought if you think you are indispensable; I could give up my other interests tomorrow.' Work was never all consuming for him; he always found time for other interests. He had been a keen sportsman from his youth. He played hockey for Trinity Hall and the YMCA Club and later organised a joint Cambridge hockey clubs tour of Switzerland. He enjoyed tennis and badminton throughout his life. For many years he was captain of the Cambridge & County Lawn Tennis Club, and he also founded and acted as secretary of the Hurst Badminton Club, chairing the county association. In 1946 he was elected as the Conservative councillor for the Trumpington Ward on Cambridge Town Council. In 1956–7 he was elected Mayor of Cambridge, which had been granted city status in 1951. At the end of his term of office he became an Alderman. Like his father before him and his sons after him, he was deeply involved with the Baptist church. He was deacon and life deacon of St Andrew's Street Baptist Church. From 1930 until 1939 he was secretary of the Cambridgeshire Baptist Association, of which he was moderator in 1947–8. He was a council member of Regent's Park College, the Baptist College in Oxford, and, from 1946 to 1953, of the Baptist Union of Great Britain and Ireland.

Ray Langford was unusual among staff in getting to know Elliot Ridgeon well. Until the garage at Cavendish Road became much busier, he was often asked to carry out little jobs for the family. He drove the boys to tennis tournaments in the Humber Super Snipe and taught all three children, David, Michael and their sister, Pat, how to drive. He also drove Elliot and his wife to the coast for their holiday, when he would be invited to take lunch with them. Elliot would quietly press a five-pound note into Ray's hand after the meal – then so would his wife. It was an extremely generous gesture, as five pounds would be worth nearly £100 today.

By the time Elliot became Mayor, he had acquired a large black Humber motorcar. It was usually confined to motoring around Cambridge on mayoral duties, while other journeys were made in his Vauxhall Wyvern. When the Humber was once used for a much longer journey, it proved unequal to the strain. Ron Coleman was driving Elliot's mother and her sister on holiday to Cromer when the car developed a water leak. As the party neared Norwich, steam began rising from the bonnet of the car. Ron's passengers disembarked, a telephone call summoned Ray in the Wyvern, in which Ron and his passengers completed their journey, leaving Ray to spend the rest of the day replacing the Humber's head gasket.

Elliot Ridgeon was a fond grandfather. He was known as 'Poppa', since his wife Joan had always called Cyril 'Pop'. His grandchildren remembered him as an upright, smartly dressed man. Although neither Elliot nor Joan was the sort of grandparent to bounce grandchildren on their knees, they were kind and interested. Gordon Ridgeon, Michael's son,

Facing page: Staff outing to Great Yarmouth, 1948, with a young Michael Ridgeon in school uniform (front, fifth from left).

Right: At Cambridge Station before the staff trip to Skegness, 1954.

Above: The Ridgeon family home,
Latham House, Trumpington Road.

remembered his grandfather taking him to the Botanic Gardens in Cambridge to feed the ducks and to a fish farm in Oxford to feed the trout. After church every Sunday the whole family would congregate at their home in Trumpington Road for Sunday lunch. Almost invariably they ate late because Joan, herself a busy woman and a leading light in Baptist church circles, particularly the Baptist Women's League, was usually late leaving church. Their house was always full of people, reflecting their busy lives and diverse interests.

Their two sons both joined the company from school, David, the elder, in 1953, followed by Michael in 1955. Both had regularly accompanied their father round the business when they were younger. Michael recalled how, at the age of six, he would pop across Tenison Road from his school to the offices during his lunch hour, and how Joyce Nunn would lift him onto a high stool where he would spend 20 happy minutes on the adding machine. His father would also take him to the mill in Cavendish Road, where Michael was fascinated by the engine room. The boys formally entered the business like any other new starter. David, born on the day of George V's Silver Jubilee in June 1935, receiving a silver cup as part of the celebrations from the town, began as a trainee in the building materials department, while Michael, born in 1937, joined the paint department under the management of Glyn Richards. The start of their careers in the company coincided with the abolition of the last of the wartime controls and the beginning of a building boom as prosperity returned. Just as Elliot Ridgeon's view of business was coloured by the

meagre days of the 1920s and 1930s, so his sons would develop a very different approach under the influence of an economic revival. David began in the Tenison Road yard under Pat Cox before studying at Cambridge Technical College. Everyone was formally addressed as Mr, Mrs or Miss (although Ray Langford and Ron Coleman remembered how almost everybody had their own nickname, such as 'Bozo', 'Gearbox' or 'Omo'). David was known as 'Mr David'. He remembered how everything was handled manually, with Rayburn cookers unloaded on to sack barrows over scaffolding boards.

Michael joined the Tenison Road showroom, where, while writing out delivery tickets, he developed the knack of translating the sometimes rather confused requests of customers: 'Head Warden's Pot' actually meant Edwardian chimney pot and 'Persecuted Hardboard' was perforated hardboard. Both David and Michael did national service. David joined the Royal Artillery in 1955 and served in Germany; Michael joined the RAF in 1956, based at Cardington, where he was in the RAF rowing crew. When David returned after two years, he worked initially at Tenison Road until the sudden death of Bill Cornell, when he replaced him as the sales representative for Ely, Downham Market and the area surrounding Cambridge, calling on small builders. In the summer of 1957 he was sent to work in a sawmill in Sweden, the first part of a year

spent studying the timber trade in Sweden and Finland. When Michael came back from the RAF, he took up a place to study architecture at Emmanuel College, Cambridge.

In 1957 the company celebrated 25 years as a limited company with a dinner for 240 people at the Guildhall in Cambridge. By now Cyril Ridgeon & Son employed more than four times as many people as it had in 1939. The company was supplying materials for the resurgence in building work in and around Cambridge. In the city itself developments included the massive Arbury Estate, complete with shops, schools and libraries, which took 15 years to complete, and various buildings for the university, while activity was also busy in the villages surrounding Cambridge. The firm was also supplying contractors working on the development of several of the so-called New Towns, including Corby and Stevenage, as well as those engaged in London on the restoration of St James's Church in Piccadilly and the House of Commons. Aga sales were booming, based mainly on the renewed prosperity of the farming industry. With open fires remaining popular, the firm continued to make tiled fireplace surrounds and even acquired a small local business, the Stukeley Slab & Tile Works, which made breezeblocks, in 1955. At the same time the firm was reacting to the encouragement of smokeless fuels and central heating as a means of combating the terrible smogs created by thousands and

Left: Emmanuel College, Cambridge, where Michael Ridgeon studied architecture.

Above: The 25-year celebration dinner at the Guildhall in Cambridge.

Top: The company directors in 1957. Back row, from left: Michael Ridgeon, portrait of Cyril Ridgeon, David Ridgeon. Front row: Leslie Ridgeon, Joan Ridgeon, Elliot Ridgeon, John Rivers and Bill Feakes.

thousands of coal fires. Peter Silk was on the road, following up leads about central heating and promoting products like Parkray stoves and room heaters.

Between the end of the war and the late 1950s the company enjoyed an almost unbroken run of increasing turnover. On the other hand, it proved difficult for the company to maintain margins in peacetime. By 1958, although sales reached £771,000, the equivalent in real terms of £13.5 million today, profits of £14,000 (£245,000) represented less than 2 per cent of turnover. This pattern was to continue during the 1960s.

'A Challenge'
1958–73

4

In 1958 Cyril Ridgeon & Son made probably its most significant acquisition, certainly the most important since the firm had been founded. The Saffron Walden Building Material Supply Company would be run by David Ridgeon as an almost entirely separate business, while his father Elliot continued to remain in charge of Cambridge.

The Saffron Walden business began in 1901 when Joseph Custerson, a former mayor of the town, started his own building firm with nine men on a small site in Station Street, selling for convenience mainly bricks and cement.

Previous pages: Traditional colourful houses in Castle Street, Saffron Walden. Saffron Walden became the third location for Ridgeons' expansion plan.

Above: Elliot Ridgeon in 1960.

Facing page: Kitchen display, Saffron Walden branch, 2010.

The construction side was separated from the materials supply side in the 1930s, when the latter became the Saffron Walden Building Material Supply Company. This became a limited company in 1947, but although the site was expanded during the 1940s and 1950s the business did not prosper. By the late 1950s the Custerson family was seeking a buyer.

When Ray Potterill began work with Custersons as a joiner's apprentice in 1955 there were about 20 employees. The Station Street premises, he remembered, were old, very cramped and overrun by rats and mice. Massive beams restricted headroom to no more than 6 feet 6 inches (190cm) so manoeuvring timber was very hard work. The sawmill in which Ray worked was typical of so many others of its time. Safety precautions were rudimentary. Bits of wood would shoot across the joiners' shop and cutters from the saws often sped past at knee-height. Wood shavings and chips were strewn everywhere, yet the only heating was provided by four gas fires. About half a dozen boys and men were employed in the shop, mainly making doors, windows and staircases. The outstanding quality of the workmanship in the joinery shop was one of the attractions for any purchaser.

One of the reasons the business was struggling, recalled Ray, was because of the extraordinary scale of the pilfering at Station Street. The boys in the mill and the shop would watch as builders walked away with bags of cement or help themselves to plumbers' accessories. 'No one bought paint.' When Alan Thompson, recently qualified as a chartered accountant, who had only joined in January 1957, prepared the accounts for that year, the business was making a substantial loss. As he recalled, it was 'unlikely to improve so it was decided the company would be sold'. It was Alan Myers, the senior partner in the firm of accountants Peters, Elseworthy & Moore that dealt with the business, who brought it to Elliot Ridgeon's attention.

David Ridgeon.

Alan Thompson.

Above left: Part of the old buildings at Station Road, showing the joiners' shop, which was located in the taller building during Custersons' time, but moved to the smaller building when Ridgeons took it over. The bell was rung twice daily, at lunchtime and closing time. Both buildings were demolished when the yard was reorganised.

Top: Board store with timber store in the background.

Above: Prepared timber and mouldings rack and fibreglass store, Station Road.

Left: Ray Potterill in the Saffron Walden workshop.

Below: Ridgeons has always prided itself on the quality of its craftsmanship.

Above: The much-improved paint department in the Saffron Walden branch today.

Above: Ridgeons fireplace display.

There were a number of reasons why Elliot Ridgeon might have been attracted by the proposition. A business in parlous condition would not have commanded a significant purchase price. Saffron Walden and its hinterland were not well covered by Ridgeons. And Elliot must surely have been thinking consciously of the future of the business. He took the decision to buy the Saffron Walden business while his son David was still in Scandinavia. When he returned home, David later recalled, his father asked him almost immediately to take over Saffron Walden. 'It was a challenge', he later recalled. He was only 23 years old and without any management experience at all. His father would come over no more often than once a week to meet David and Alan Thompson. But Elliot himself had taken over the effective management of the business from his own father when he was only a little older than his son. He clearly saw this as the best way to test his son and allow him to develop his own style, away from Cambridge and his own influence. For a man who generally liked to have the final say in everything that went on at Cambridge, it was a very open-minded

approach. It was also a calculated decision, for the stakes involved at Saffron Walden were not high; the business could scarcely decline any further. The mere fact of the purchase had given an immediate boost to its fortunes. The connection with Ridgeons opened doors to new suppliers on much more beneficial terms, brought the services of skilled timber buyers and gave the business the financial backing it needed to secure cash discounts and eliminate its previous reputation as a financial risk.

Elliot was probably a better judge of his son's capabilities than David was himself. Alan Thompson recalled the immediate difference created by David Ridgeon's assumption of the role of managing director, saying that he created a positive mood, making himself known to all the staff, gauging their skills and strengths, always generous with praise and thanks. Alan Thompson later remembered how 'we now had someone who cared, who knew his job and obviously intended that we were to be successful. By circulating around the yard, he made himself known to our customers, large and small, and was soon on speaking terms and able to recognise them. Doubtless our customers took advantage of this to have a moan if something displeased them. This was a very positive thing to happen.'

It was daunting for David Ridgeon. He had little experience and no training, relied heavily on his natural instincts and was guided by principles derived from his Christian faith. He made an effort to know people's names because, he felt, 'you can't go and talk to people and not know their names'. He also believed in seeking consensus, believing that 'if you dictate what you want, often it just won't happen'.

It took a year just to bring the business back onto an even keel financially. When David Ridgeon arrived, he found most mornings that Alan Thompson was receiving writs for the recovery of debts. The business was also saddled with old buildings in serious need of maintenance and modernisation. In spite of this, the business had potential. The commitment of long-serving and experienced staff was invaluable in helping to turn the business round. These included Winnie Davies, Les Camp, Eric Page, Ray Potterill, Ralph Porter, Albert Ridgewell, Alfie Wrankmor, Titch Barker, Alan Thompson and Ted Ellis. The firm also began capitalising on the lack of serious local competition and slowly started pushing the boundaries of its sales territory deeper into Essex. David Ridgeon took the Cambridge business as his template and benefited through having many products delivered from Cambridge to Saffron Walden.

Building up the business took time, and until it was possible to reinvest in better premises the firm remained in Station Road. When Arthur Swan joined the firm in 1960, followed by Jack Goddard in the next year, they found that in the yard you were covered in dust in the summer and up to your knees in mud in the winter. Marion Smith, who first came to the firm in 1967, remembers a ramshackle, higgledy-piggledy building, where you could hear the mice running along the loft and, when it rained, you knew exactly where to place the buckets to collect the water leaking through the roof.

Yet there was steady progress as David Ridgeon built up the business bit by bit. In 1959, adjacent premises were acquired where concrete pipes had once been made and, even further back, mineral waters had been produced. A cement and plaster shed was erected. Also in 1959, a business premises in the same street was acquired and the old stables were turned into a sanitaryware store. As a result, Percy Bassett joined the firm and, with Jack Goddard, he helped to build up the new sanitaryware department. Percy, no longer a young man, was renowned for his ability to leap a trade counter without touching it.

The paint and ironmongery department was run by Fred Clayden, assisted by Arthur Swan, his eventual successor.

Above: Fred Clayden, manager of the paint and ironmongery department until his death in 1972.

Left: Yard at the back of Station Road.

Top: The showroom at Saffron Walden, 1960.

Then and now: bathroom displays in the Saffron Walden branch in the 1960s (above left) and today (above right).

Arthur remembered Fred as a manager of the old school, stocking everything in cardboard boxes, each one labelled with the selling price and – in hieroglyphics only Fred understood – the cost price. Paint and ironmongery was the first department to be modernised, located above a new showroom for the tile surrounds and bathrooms, and both were given an official opening in December 1960 with the aim of raising the profile of the business. After sherry, the mayor officially opened the revitalised premises, and the evening concluded with more refreshments. Pictures show a bright, clean, unfussy frontage with various units on display behind a large plate-glass window.

Further properties were acquired nearby as trade grew. The former Co-op coal yard was purchased in 1963 for the display of sheds, greenhouses and paving slabs and stock of Calor Gas cylinders. For extra storage the firm leased both the old engine shed at the station and the disused cinema and carpark. Eventually the firm owned or rented almost the

THE DIRECTORS
of the
SAFFRON WALDEN BUILDING MATERIAL SUPPLY CO. LTD.
request the pleasure of the company of

_____

on the occasion of the opening of their

NEW SHOWROOMS
(STATION STREET)

by His Worship the Mayor of Saffron Walden
(Alderman S. S. Wilson, J.P.)

THURSDAY, DECEMBER 8th, 1960

Sherry 6.30 p.m.   Official Opening 7.15 p.m., followed by films.
Refreshments 8.30 p.m.

R.S.V.P. by 1st December, 1960

The opening of the Station Street showroom at Saffron Walden, 1960. From left: Mrs Eileen Thompson, Alan Thompson, Mrs Kitty Wilson, David Ridgeon, The Mayor, Alderman Stanley Wilson, Mrs Joan Ridgeon and Cyril Ridgeon.

Above: Invitation card for the opening.

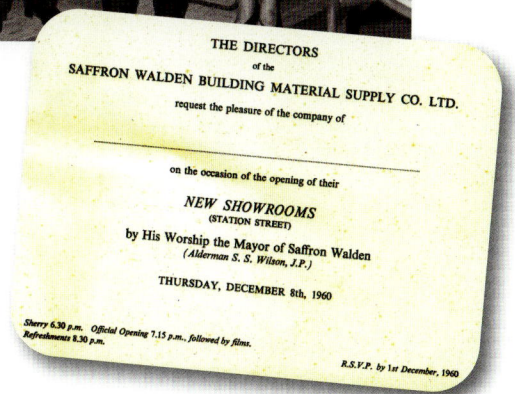

whole of Station Street. In 1965 the paint and ironmongery department was extended and a new heating department was opened. The latter was needed to cope with the growing demand for central heating systems. It featured multi-storey racks serviced by a forklift truck, reflecting David Ridgeon's interest in utilising modern technology. Peter Lawrence, with several years' experience in the trade, had been recruited the year previously as manager. As space became even more congested in Station Street, the retail hardware department was moved out in 1965 to a purpose-built

Top: Forklift trucks are commonplace in warehouses today but were considered cutting-edge technology in the 1960s.

Above: The introduction of mechanical handling of goods was a welcome addition to the Station Street headquarters. One innovation was the Lloyleva self-adjusting loading platform which made the deliveries of goods to and

from the depot much easier. Seen unloading goods onto the platform is Alfie Wrankmor, a former prisoner of war and long-time employee of Ridgeons, who used to walk the length of the heating store on his hands every day.

Top right: Percy Bassett moves heavy heating equipment to the top rack of the stores using the forklift truck of the day.

property in the Market Square, trading as Gayhomes, a name chosen from staff suggestions. Not only was the new store much more accessible for customers, it featured self-service, still a novelty at the time, as well as piped music and a speaker system used for advertising and information. At Station Street the vacated space was filled with more displays of fireplaces, boilers, bathrooms and kitchens. David Ridgeon, following the principle embraced at Cambridge, was keen to make sure that customers could always find what they wanted. His policy of creating separate departments, along the lines of the Cambridge business, helped staff to provide more individual advice to customers. They were all encouraged to study the technical aspects of products and services and take trade qualifications. By 1965 the firm had increased the number of people it employed to 60, a threefold rise in seven years, reflecting just how much progress it was making. By the early 1970s the staff total had risen to 85.

This was achieved as much in the field as it was in the departments in Station Street. James Williams joined the paint and ironmongery department in 1961, and was sent out on the road by David Ridgeon two years later. James covered a wide territory, including the areas between Saffron Walden and Cambridge, bounded by Haverhill, as far as Royston and beyond Bishop's Stortford. Although he was supposed to be a specialist paints and ironmongery salesman, he took orders for any products from customers. This caused some trouble at first as timber, for instance, was outside his experience, but he received strong support from older staff at Station Street. He opened up many new accounts and came to know the families of many customers very well, often being invited to stay for lunch or tea.

Orders were delivered from Saffron Walden by the firm's small fleet of lorries. Eddie Izard, who joined Saffron Walden in 1964, became a driver as soon as he was old enough to pass the driving test and has loved the job ever since. This was a time when drivers operated along defined routes, and Eddie would travel out to Steeple Bumpstead one day, and do the run to Linton the next. He too came to know many of his customers very well and, as David Ridgeon would later remark, he 'knew where the best cups of tea were made'. One customer, when a ton of cement had been loaded into a shed, tipped Eddie with half a crown. The transport manager at Saffron Walden was Peter

Below left: A new retail shop was opened in Market Square in 1966, under the name Gayhomes. The store name was chosen from a list submitted by staff members.

Below right: Display of kitchen equipment inside the store.

Bottom: Staff members. Back row from left: Arthur Swan, Ron Hunt, Peter Lawrence, Peter Young and Henry Cranwell. Front row: Tony Davey, Ted Ellis, David Ridgeon and Jack Goddard.

Below: Saffron Walden's transport fleet in 1956, which comprised two Bedford articulated vehicles, five Bedford lorries, one fitted with a tail-lift and two Ford Transit trucks.

Young, who joined in 1958 and also looked after the yard. A well-known character in the trade, Peter was renowned for looking after his customers and for his knowledge of building regulations.

David Ridgeon, supported by Alan Thompson, created a place where people enjoyed coming to work. David Ridgeon's office door was always open and he put everyone at ease. He regularly walked around the site and, although he could be very sharp if something was not in order, he was always very fair. Ray Potterill remembered David Ridgeon bearing down on him, frown on his face, only to move on without saying a word as he realised that what he thought was a cigarette hanging from Ray's lips was in fact the stub of his white pencil. Unlike his father, David would review staff wages and conditions regularly without being asked. Sincere and caring, his example, remembered Peter Lawrence, rubbed off on many staff. David Ridgeon was always very supportive of his managers, and James Williams was among those who appreciated how he was trusted with new opportunities and increased responsibilities as his career developed. He also remembered Alan Thompson as a wonderful man, who 'never found a fault or had a bad

thing to say about anybody'. Although Thompson was principally the accountant, he had a huge panel of sample brick facings in his office and never missed the opportunity to sell to a customer. He had an unusual filing system, consisting of large piles of papers dotted around his office, but from which he could retrieve anything he was asked for. Staff members were rather more in awe of Elliot Ridgeon, as they were at Cambridge. When he arrived for his weekly visit, usually on a Wednesday, the shout would often go up, 'Elliot's about!' so that people could keep out of his way.

For David Ridgeon, the first really significant development at Saffron Walden was the building in 1968 of a new mill and timber store on the Shirehill industrial estate in the town. 'Double handling' had been inevitable at Station Street because the layout was so inefficient; this was resolved by building a large timber store at Shirehill. The new store was so huge that David's father referred to it as Ely Cathedral, and it was built so that it could be converted easily into a mezzanine warehouse. Within an existing building at Shirehill a modern sawmill was created. By now the fleet of delivery vehicles numbered nine and orders made prior to 4pm one day were sent out the next. In 1973, when the timber store and yard were both extended, a new joiners' shop was provided. When the men moved from Station Street, they found a modern building properly

Top: In 1968 a piece of land was leased on the Shirehill industrial estate to erect a new sawmill with timber storage facilities (above). On completion, the Timber machinery and stock was transferred from Station Street to the new site on Shirehill.

Right: The new warehouse boasted a capacity of 195 tons of timber. One innovation was a side-loading mobile racking system consisting of a series of racks mounted on bases which ran in special tracks let into the floor. With the former pigeon-hole style racks, it was not possible to gauge the length of a piece of timber without unloading it first. Timber withdrawn by mistake thus tended to end up discarded on the floor. The open construction of the new racks made it much easier to identify the lengths of the timber at a glance, saving time and labour costs.

Clockwise from, top: In 1961 Ridgeons celebrated its Golden Jubilee. Open days and tours formed part of the celebrations. Michael Ridgeon shows visitors round the Tenison Road yard; The directors outside the Tenison Road office, 1961; Directors and staff also marked the occasion with a dinner at the Dorothy Café; The Jubilee Seal, created from a sketch by Mr Nunn, who won a competition to come up with a suitable design. The prize was awarded for 'ingenuity, tidiness and suitability'.

heated and equipped with extraction plant. Here Ray Potterill eventually took over as shop foreman from Ralph Porter, and the shop carried out orders for builders as far away as Lowestoft.

Despite the links with Ridgeons, there was always a keen rivalry between Cambridge and Saffron Walden, where staff were fiercely proud of their independence. In Cambridge, where sometimes it seemed as if little would ever change, some members of staff were envious of the developments they saw at Saffron Walden.

In 1961 the Cambridge business celebrated its 50th anniversary; in the same year turnover exceeded £1 million

for the first time. During May and June open days were held for customers and, in October, the Dorothy Café again hosted a staff dinner. Ray Cornell – whose father had made a similar presentation to Cyril Ridgeon 25 years before – presented Elliot Ridgeon, on behalf of the directors and staff, with a gold cigarette case. David and Michael Ridgeon each received a clock following their marriages, David to Jill Starling and Michael to Penny Powell. In November another dinner was held, this time for civic, university and trade guests, at the University Arms. Colonel John Jewson, of the famous timber dynasty, proposed the toast, recollecting that his father had traded with Cyril. Elliot Ridgeon joked that

Jewson really should have come along with an irresistible takeover bid.

No business could reach half a century by standing still. Change was taking place in Cambridge, even though it came rather piecemeal and lacked the sense of purpose seen in Saffron Walden. This was partly because the business, too focused on turnover, was generating insufficient profits for reinvestment (they averaged less than 2 per cent of sales until 1970) and Elliot Ridgeon was unwilling to borrow.

In 1959, after more than 30 years, the steam-powered, belt-driven system of powering machinery in the mill at Cavendish Road, was finally replaced with individual electric motors for each machine. In the same year the company took new premises at 20 Regent Street, with accommodation spread over four floors, in a central location opposite the University Arms Hotel posing few parking problems at that time. Elliot Ridgeon knew the property was coming up for auction but also knew that, since it backed onto the grounds of Downing College, the college authorities were likely to be interested. He struck a deal with the college bursar in advance of the auction, agreeing not to compete for the property in exchange for taking a lease on it.

Leslie Ridgeon, who loved displays and liked things to be smart, excelled himself at Regent Street. He had seen the London showroom of Allied Ironfounders and decided the company should have one just as fine. The Regent Street showrooms, complete with fishpond in the semi-basement, were regarded, recalled David Ridgeon, 'as quite out of this world at the time'. Opened in March 1959, with 5,000 square feet of display space, they featured bathrooms on the lower ground floor, tiled fireplace surrounds on the ground floor and kitchens on the first floor. On one occasion two young children made use of the toilets on display while their horrified parents were being served. A number of young men who began their careers with Ridgeons at Regent Street remember the hand-wound lift, with the winding-gear housed in a small room no more than 5 feet high. Ray Andrus, who joined the company in 1962, recalled how there were competitions to see who could be the fastest to wind the lift up to the top of the building.

Elliot Ridgeon, unlike his son, had to be persuaded of the merit of mechanical handling. As road haulage became more sophisticated and forklift trucks were required to shift goods loaded onto pallets, he responded to the suggestion put to him by John Doggett that the company should buy

Above: The shop exterior, 20 Regent Street.

Right: Displays inside the showroom were a grand affair and an extension of the attractive displays in the shop window, showing off top-of-the-range bathrooms and fireplace surrounds.

these machines by asking, 'Don't your men want to work?' When Doggett told him the alternative was higher haulage charges, he conceded the point. The first forklift was introduced in 1961 for handling timber at Cavendish Road. It remained the only one in Cambridge until at least 1969. For Peter Silk, forklifts would transform working practices. While a single delivery of thousands of loose bricks took several hours to unload by hand, a forklift truck could unload a lorry-load of pallets in just half an hour. Hydraulic tail-lifts were also fitted to lorries carrying larger goods, such as fireplace surrounds and baths. So too were Hiab cranes, after considerable discussion as to whether they should be fitted behind the cab or at the back of the lorry.

There was no forklift at Tenison Road when John Shepherd began work there in 1969. One of his first jobs was to unload warm cement by hand, using a sack barrow and gloves. Three years later nails were still arriving at the yard in heavy hessian sacks, five staff lining up between lorry and counter, throwing the sacks from one to the other. For Ivor Muncey, a new starter in 1972, aged only 17, it was a daunting experience to find a sack, nails poking out of it, being hurled towards you.

A new heating department had been opened at Cavendish Road in 1963, although for the next five years it was housed temporarily in an ancient building. This was popularly known as the 'Fowl House' because it had once been a chicken house. It had been taken down and re-erected on site by Leslie Wedd of Wedd & Sons in 1943, when licences for building or materials were almost impossible to obtain. When the department moved into a new store in 1968, the question arose about what to do with the 'Fowl House'. Tony Davis, who joined the firm as

heating manager in 1967, remembers suggesting to Elliot Ridgeon that it was fit only for demolition. Elliot was indignant: 'Davis, anyone can give things away!'

Like his father, Elliot Ridgeon was particularly interested in timber. For many years the company had shared timber shipments and transport with other firms since Ridgeons was not officially recognised as an independent importer, a status jealously guarded by members of the Timber Trade Federation (TTF). Elliot had always wanted the company to buy timber through agents as well as brokers and other merchants and finally won status as an importer from the TTF in the early 1960s. Ridgeons initially took advantage of the efficient service and low handling charges offered by the port at Felixstowe and in 1963 negotiated terms for ships' discharge, unloading onto transport and cartage to rented storage areas. The timber came in coasters, mainly under the German flag, from Sweden and Finland. The container revolution changed all this. In 1968 Felixstowe informed timber importers that timber could be accepted only for through-transit on ro-ro vessels. The company made alternative arrangements, eventually using a wharf on the Colne at

Rowhedge, downstream from Colchester, opposite Wivenhoe. As at Felixstowe, the National Dock Labour Scheme did not apply there, a considerable advantage when many ports suffered from strikes. The shipping revolution also led to Ridgeons ceasing to use the Surrey Docks, taking North American softwood instead from Tilbury, Newport and Cardiff. Softwoods were also imported through King's Lynn and were taken by rail to Cavendish Road. British Rail made an effort to modernise when so many operators began using forklift trucks, but the flatbed trucks they introduced in place of common user wagons were often unavailable for Ridgeons. It seemed symptomatic of the decline of the railways that in November 1964 the coal chute erected at Tenison Road in 1932 was demolished. With rail no longer practical or economic, the Cavendish Road siding was taken up and every load of timber came by road. This in itself created another problem, causing increasing congestion along Cavendish Road and consequent irritation among local residents.

By the late 1960s Mick Rowell had become the yard manager at Cavendish Road, while Bill Feakes remained director with responsibility for timber. Steve Lee, who joined Ridgeons in 1967 and moved to Cavendish Road in 1969, remembered Feakes as a firm but fair man, typical, in fact, of many senior managers. Although fiery in temperament, someone who never tolerated fools kindly, he never held a grudge. He was respected for his integrity. He would never put himself in a situation where there was a potential conflict of interest. For instance, he never accepted lunch invitations from customers.

March remained the only Ridgeons branch outside Cambridge, other than Saffron Walden, which still traded as an independent business. A new showroom was opened at March on 1 February 1963. This was in the middle of severe winter weather, but although snow and frozen roads prevented the attendance of directors from Cambridge, some 150 customers and their wives still attended the event. The company was selling almost as many paraffin lamps as it could find, more often than not for use as heaters to keep the outside toilets, still common in many British homes, from freezing. During the freeze, Ray Andrus remembered cycling with a friend from work down to the Cam at lunchtime, taking their skates and spending an hour skating along the river. A year later the Broad Street shop in March was finally closed, with operations transferred to new premises built at Creek Road. Among the staff was Dick Pinning, who joined as a 15-year-old straight from school in 1958 and retired 45 years later due to ill health. As office junior, he did everything, including lighting the fire in the manager's office every morning. When four of the six staff members were absent one day, watching a football match at Norwich, he was left alone to unload 10 tons of cement by hand. When he went home, his neck was covered with blisters from the hot cement.

Above: Ray Andrus.

Left: Skating on the River Cam during the 'big freeze' of 1963.

Ridgeons did make one acquisition during the 1960s. The opportunity had been brought to Elliot Ridgeon's attention by Alan Myers, who also, earlier on, had pointed out Saffron Walden to him. This time the business was Frank Unwin's building and joinery firm in Histon whose son had emigrated to Australia. In 1966 Ridgeons acquired the joinery side with the retail shop in Station Road, Histon. There were many long standing members of staff, some 30 joiners plus Howard (office manager), Carmichael (accounts), Knights (estimator), Hudson (shop foreman), Travel (shop manager), Love (supply and fix and other works) and finally Eric Wakefield (representative). The company produced an extensive range of high quality joinery from staircases, bar counters and booths to bookcases, cocktail cabinets, wardrobes and pews.

In 1965 Ridgeons, on the initiative of Michael Ridgeon, also took over the Calor Gas agency previously held by King & Harper, a local motor dealer, recruiting King & Harper's existing manager, Bill Hall. Calor Gas appliances were originally displayed at Hobson Street, with the cylinders held at Cavendish Road, from where they were distributed. The slabbing shop making tiled surrounds eventually closed as central heating became more popular than open fires. The service was also extended to Saffron Walden, where Bacon's fish and chip shop was taken over for the purpose.

There were lots of other small changes affecting Ridgeons during the 1960s, often stemming from changes in the industry. In the mid-1960s Formica, once such a common covering on kitchen surfaces, was introduced, and its popularity led the company to set up a separate Formica department. Kitchen planning, whose potential Elliot Ridgeon had foreseen in the early 1950s when it was almost unheard of, became increasingly popular. Manufacturers began producing kitchen cabinets and wall cupboards, and the result was the concept of the fitted kitchen. By 1971 Saffron Walden had already introduced a kitchen design service, offering easy payment terms. At Regent Street kitchen units, as with most other retailers, came ready assembled, but by the early 1970s the flatpack revolution was imminent. Plastics were being used more and more, for everything from rainwater goods and drainage to baths. In 1971 Ridgeons first began ordering plastic goods from Osma, a relationship that still continues. Emulsion paint transformed decorating, replacing distemper and eroding the popularity of wallpaper.

In 1966 the company adopted a punched card system for invoicing and statements, although this was superseded in the late 1970s when the company began using computers. On the trade counters mental arithmetic was employed for calculations, even after the introduction of less expensive electronic calculators, which were regarded by some older hands with mistrust.

Right: The inauguration of the 25 Club, held at the University Arms Hotel on 6 October 1958. Employees who had completed 25 or more years' service were treated to dinner, followed by presentations of club badges and gifts such as inscribed gold wrist watches or clocks as rewards for their years of loyal service to the company.

Below: Bill Feakes and Vic Keys (below middle) receive their awards from Joan Ridgeon.

Below right: Michael Ridgeon performed his magic act with members of the Pentacle Club to entertain the guests.

Working conditions remained much the same. At Tenison Road men still had their breaks or ate their lunch just inside the yard gate, in a mess hut containing two benches and an Aga. Cheese sandwiches brought from home and toasted on the Aga were popular. When Tony Davis first began working at Cavendish Road in 1967 he found the washing facilities limited to a bucket for washing hands, which often froze overnight in winter. At Tenison Road the men's toilets were prevented from freezing up only by keeping a paraffin stove lit. The thick atmosphere it produced was not helped by all the smoking that went on, since this, with the mess hut, was one of only two places where smoking was permitted. Ivor Muncey described the site as 'a set of corrugated tin huts'. Pay was still not regularly reviewed. Jimmy Nunn recalled that, over time, he had received three offers to move elsewhere. On each occasion Elliot Ridgeon agreed to match the pay he had been offered to keep him with the company. This, reflected Jimmy, was almost the only way to get a pay rise. Elliot Ridgeon's action, on the other hand, did show that he valued the contribution made by capable staff with the rise of an old penny per hour being the norm. The distinction between white-collar and blue-collar staff remained. When Nigel Haslop joined the company in 1971, earning £8 a week, office staff enjoyed a lunch break 15 minutes longer than yard staff.

Top left: Leslie Ridgeon retired in 1968. He is pictured (centre) with Mrs Joan Ridgeon and Peter Silk.

Top right: Alan Butler, Bill Feakes and Arthur Chapman.

Above: Other long-serving members of staff with spouses include (from left): Stan Haynes, Bill Whitmore, Mrs Whitmore, Mrs Stone and Sid Stone.

One change was the introduction of a five-day working week for office staff by the mid-1960s. When the government began to push for increased training throughout industry, the company could point to its well-established commitment, from product training for heating department staff and courses on Aga cookers to the attendance of apprentices one day a week on courses held at the technical college and the general encouragement of staff to take the various courses offered by the National Federation of Builders' and Plumbers' Merchants, now the Builders' Merchants' Federation.

The company retained the loyalty of so many staff that a club for members with 25 or more years of service was formed on 6 October 1958 with a dinner at the University Arms Hotel. Sid Stone was the first chairman of the 25 Club, as it was called. For several years the club often held social evenings with other clubs, such as King & Harper, the Co-op and the Railway Social Club. When the club held its dinner in 1960, the entertainment came from Michael Ridgeon and his fellow magicians from the Cambridge University Pentacle Club.

In 1958 staff from Cambridge and Saffron Walden joined forces for an annual outing by special train to London. Further trips to the capital took place in 1960 and 1962. In 1959 the destination was Skegness, but there was no outing during 1961 because of the Golden Jubilee celebrations. The 1962 outing proved to be the last, as the logistics of transporting so many people became increasingly complicated. From 1963 onwards the outing was replaced by an annual dinner, the first one held, as ever, in the Dorothy Café. At first these were held jointly but from 1966 onwards the lack of a large enough space locally meant that Cambridge and Saffron Walden each organised their own events.

At Cambridge Elliot Ridgeon continued to manage the company in much the same way. When John Rivers and Leslie Ridgeon retired in 1968, Alan Thompson was asked to take on the duties of chief accountant at Cambridge, in addition to his work at Saffron Walden. Ivor Warren was also appointed an executive director in 1968, with responsibility for timber transport and shipping. Peter Silk was appointed general manager, also assuming the responsibilities previously undertaken by Michael Ridgeon, who had accepted his vocation to become a Baptist minister. Michael had struggled to resist this call for several years, since serving in the RAF, feeling bound to serve in the family business. When he finally revealed his dilemma to his father one day at the office, Elliot told Michael that he had known something was troubling him and that he should go home and they would talk in the evening. When they did, Elliot told his son that he would have the committed support of his family in his new direction in life, something that his brother David also pledged. In August 1967 Michael left the company to study at Regent's Park Baptist College in Oxford.

By the early 1970s the Cambridge and Saffron Walden businesses together were turning over more than £4.5m (£45m today, taking into account changes in the RPI). In real terms the business had grown threefold since the late 1950s. Profits continued to lag behind turnover, and sank away almost to nothing in the late 1960s, but at the end of 1972 they had exceeded 7 per cent of turnover for the first time since the late 1940s. Like many others in the sector, the company benefited from the construction boom of the early 1970s. Although the economic situation was worsening, dominated by rising inflation and strikes in the mines and at the docks, Ridgeons appeared to be moving in the right direction.

'A Real Gentleman'
1973–84

5

AT THE BEGINNING OF 1973 Elliot Ridgeon announced that his son would begin assuming responsibility for management at Cambridge in preparation for Elliot's retirement. As it turned out, the transition was short, for Elliot died after a long illness on 19 July 1973 at the age of 69. 'His patience and cheerfulness through his suffering,' wrote Ivor Warren, 'impressed all those who visited him.' Despite the announcement concerning David, Elliot's death caused some uncertainty among Cambridge staff, who had little experience of David's style of management and knew little of his intentions. This was quickly dispelled. David Ridgeon's success in transforming the Saffron Walden business had given him a clear view of the direction he had in mind for Ridgeons.

Previous pages: Ridgeons lorries offloading sand at the Nuffield Road branch.

Facing page: The Ridgeon family has a long association with St Andrew's Street Baptist Church. Cyril served here as deacon and secretary, generations of family marriages were solemnised here, and the service for Elliot's funeral was conducted here in 1973.

Right: Elliot Ridgeon (centre), receiving his special silver log and gold axe on a plinth from David and Michael representing 25 and 50 years' service respectively. From left: Penny Ridgeon, Michael Ridgeon, Joan Ridgeon, David Ridgeon and Jill Ridgeon.

Economically, it was not an easy time to take charge of a business that required modernisation. The economic conditions of the 1970s and 1980s were unsettled. In the mid-1970s the UK suffered a collapse in the property market, the secondary banking crisis and a steep rise in oil prices, all of which contributed towards rampant inflation and industrial strife. During the second half of the 1970s economic growth was half the rate achieved during the 1960s. Then came the slump of the early 1980s with the evaporation of economic growth and soaring unemployment. The only positive indicator was a steep fall in both the rate of inflation and the incidence of strikes. Yet throughout these torrid times Ridgeons recorded rising turnover and a consistent increase in profits. By 1984 the company was making sales of more than £38m (worth more than £92m today, based on changes in the RPI), with profits of £2.3m (£5.5m today). More importantly, profits were consistently above 5 per cent of sales. The company was enjoying the most sustained period of growth in its history and earning sufficient profits to reinvest in further growth.

David Ridgeon's leadership was a key factor in this achievement. His management style had as big an impact on staff in Cambridge as it had had on staff in Saffron Walden. The verdict of one employee, that David Ridgeon was 'a real gentleman', was widely shared. Charmed by his politeness and courtesy, most staff would do anything for him. His general approach was encapsulated in the remarks he made for the staff handbook in 1979. 'The success of a business such as ours relies heavily on the quality of our staff and to the service we give to our customers. Service does not mean only prompt delivery of orders, but courtesy and helpfulness over the telephone, the counter and at the point of delivery.' He believed every member of staff should be offered training to enhance their value to the business. 'I believe as an employer that if I am to expect high standards of performance from my staff, then the company must encourage and assist you.' David Ridgeon stressed the importance of consensus, noting that staff would always be consulted over major changes to working conditions but emphasising how 'it has always been the custom of the company that any member of the staff may, if they feel it justifiable, see me about any matter they wish'.

Equally importantly, David was quite happy to delegate responsibility to his senior managers, so long as they kept him informed, creating a management team consisting partly of existing employees who had made progress through the company and partly of talented outsiders. He made significant changes within his first year in charge. While Peter Silk and Bill Feakes continued in their previous roles, they were joined, as executive directors, by Tony Davis and Peter Lawrence. Davis was responsible for

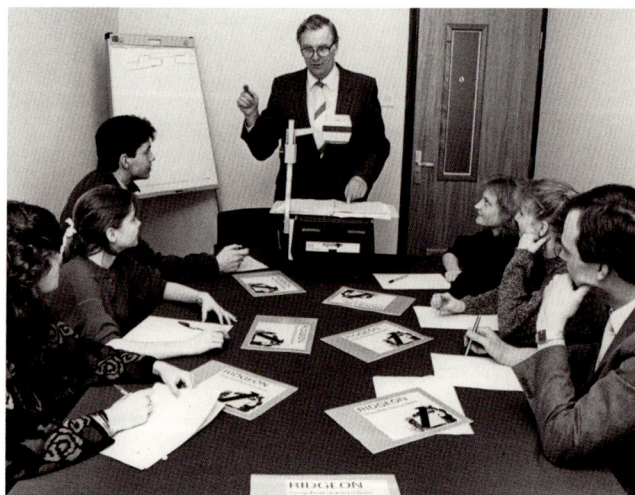

Above: Training session at Saffron Walden, led by Neville Ogley, c.1981.

Left: Tenison Road, c.1974. From left: Mike Symons, Peter Silk, David Ridgeon, Bill Feakes and Ivor Warren.

heating, assisted by his able secretary, Pat Pagram (later Terry Parker's secretary), and Lawrence for Saffron Walden, which David Ridgeon continued to visit regularly. Two key posts were filled from outside the company. Mike Symons, a qualified chartered accountant, was appointed company accountant in 1973, reporting to Alan Thompson. Within a year he had been appointed an executive director. Derrick Brook, with considerable experience at other builders' merchants, including Marlows and Travis & Arnold, both rivals of Ridgeons, was appointed as Group Sales Coordinator to create an effective sales and marketing function. Derrick was appointed an executive director in 1977. He was assisted by James Williams, an internal appointee to Field Sales Manager in 1974. James would go on to become an executive director in 1981. The executive team met monthly under David Ridgeon's chairmanship, another innovation. Family directors took no part in the day-to-day management of the business, for which the executive directors were jointly responsible, David Ridgeon acting as a link between them. The line of command was very short, for beneath David Ridgeon and his team were just the managers and the rest of the staff.

Michael Symons did much to modernise the company's approach to finance. A long overdue step was providing managers for the first time with departmental budgets. Another was the replacement of the punched card system with computerised accounts, initially prepared by an

Clockwise from top left:
Computerised accounts at Tenison
Road; Computers in the office, Ken
Miller, Viv Storey (née Price) and

Christine French, c.1980; Mike
Symons; Tony Davis; Peter
Lawrence.

external computer bureau and then from 1980 by the company's first computer system. Beginning with 16 terminals, this was a revelation and of fundamental importance in managing the business. It revealed, for instance, the difference in profitability between goods collected by the customer and those delivered by the company, leading to a conscious decision by the company to maintain the latter for their importance as part of the service to the customer.

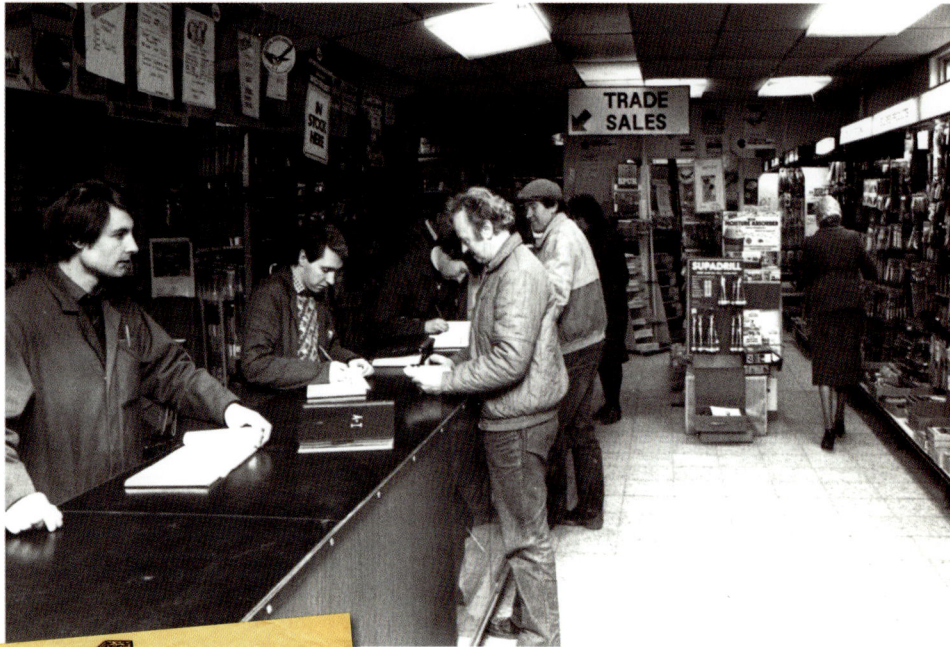

We can now supply from stock —
Solid Fuel Boilers • Gas Boilers Oil Boilers
AGA COOKERS • RAYBURN COOKERS CONVECTOR FIRES
Tiled Surrounds • Kitchen Units BENDIX WASHERS
BATHROOM SUITES and ACCESSORIES
Full range of IRONMONGERY and CARSON'S PAINTS
Timber and all General Building Materials
VISIT OUR SHOWROOMS
CYRIL RIDGEON & SON LTD.
11, CREEK ROAD (Tel. 2013) **MARCH**

Derrick Brook's influence on sales and marketing was enormous. He relished the challenge of developing something almost from scratch. He recalled the long pause at his interview when he asked about the advertising budget – it did not exist. On arriving at Tenison Road in 1974, he wondered whether he had done the right thing. The premises were substandard wooden buildings on a large piece of open land, where the floodwater formed puddles large enough to attract the ducks. With the site held only on an annual lease, there was little incentive to change, and its appearance had remained much the same for years. There was little evidence of mechanical handling: everything was still being done by hand. Overall, 'everything was archaic and out of date'. While there were many loyal customers, there were also many who were critical of the business, its poor facilities, lack of competitiveness and attitude towards service, which had become casual. Brook's objectives meshed entirely with those of David Ridgeon. Over a period of two or three years the culture of service was revived, winning over most of the company's critical customers and regaining many of those who had gone elsewhere. The sales force at Cambridge and Saffron Walden was entirely reorganised, with comprehensive objectives given to specialist representatives for the first time. A small print room was set up at Tenison Road, and advertisements for the company began to appear in local newspapers, part of a policy of raising the profile of the business and encouraging new custom. The lull provided by the dismal economic conditions was helpful, giving the company some breathing space in which to become more competitive – something that busier times would not have permitted.

This team worked together through the 1970s and early 1980s on the many changes that transformed and diversified the company's activities. The first of several completely new ventures was CRS Wholesale (Cambridge) Ltd, which carried out wholesale distribution on behalf of sanitaryware suppliers. It originated in 1976 through a casual conversation at the National Merchants' Buying Society trade fair between David Ridgeon and Bill Harris of Coopers of Oxford. Both their businesses were members of the Combined Buyers Association, a group of independent merchants pooling their buying power. They discussed the difficulties of one manufacturer, Shires, which advertised heavily but always seemed unable to match supply with demand. As a result, David Ridgeon persuaded Shires to allow Ridgeons to stock their baths and other sanitaryware on a wholesale basis. The name of the new business was intended to indicate that it was completely separate from the rest of the company to prevent any conflict of interest with existing customers.

It began in September 1976 under the part-time management of Terry Parker, with one part-time representative, utilising staff from elsewhere in the company for loading and unloading. With the help of the manufacturers' representatives, Derrick Brook worked hard to promote sales to other merchants and High Street bathroom outlets. With so many new small customers, CRS Wholesale's experience proved a helpful lesson in credit control for Ridgeons. Originally located on the Coral Park Estate in

Coldhams Lane, Cambridge, the business moved to Cavendish Road in December 1978, when the 'Fowl House' was finally removed to make way for a new building to house both CRS Wholesale and Ridgeons' own heating and sanitary department. A full-time manager, John Saunders, with extensive experience at other merchants, was recruited. The new building remained as prone to flooding as the one it had replaced, for nothing had been done to alleviate the difference in levels of more than 3 metres between the top and bottom of the site. When there was heavy rain, water poured down the carpark towards the building, sending staff scuttling out to move boxes inside.

CRS Wholesale quickly covered East Anglia and the north and east of London, reaching Peterborough, Stamford and the Norfolk coast. Early success came partly because the new business drew on the strengths of its parent. CRS Wholesale worked closely with customers, helping to set up trade shows and putting on courses in association with suppliers. From a small number of pastel colours, which had remained the same since the 1950s, there was an explosion in the range of colours available during the 1970s and 1980s, as well as a growing number of permutations for many items. But delivery times could be abysmal, with some products taking up to 20 weeks. In times of short supply, CRS Wholesale would buy products from other distributors in order to keep customers satisfied. Stockholding could be complex, but CRS Wholesale had

Above: CRS Wholesale, built on the site of the former 'Fowl House' at Cavendish Road.

Left: Terry Parker, who had worked for Ridgeons since 1965, was the first manager of CRS Wholesale.

Far left: CRS Wholesale staff.

Above: Ridgehire's first customer, Ian Jerram, with future director David Bryan (then branch manager) at Cromwell Road.

Top and above: Ridgehire, Ridgeons' plant hire business, was started in 1977 and based initially at Cavendish Road, later branching out to Saffron Walden.

(DIY), but instead the business drew most of its revenue from trade customers reluctant to invest in items of plant they would use only rarely. In 1977 a plant hire department was opened in Saffron Walden, taking over the former fish and chip shop and vegetable store in Station Street.

DIY was beginning to make an impact. The trendsetter had been B&Q, whose first store had opened in Southampton in 1969, with another 25 following during the next ten years. David Ridgeon was keen to enter the growing market for DIY from the moment he took over in Cambridge. Although the idea was causing consternation in the trade, with many operators lukewarm in the face of hostility from builders, David Ridgeon believed resistance was futile. There was a popular demand for DIY. People wanted to buy packaged goods, of the right size, which they could see on the shelf, take away and fit. On a fact-finding expedition to Australia with the British Hardware Federation, David discovered that the Australians were a long way ahead of the British in developing the idea. He returned more than ever convinced of DIY's future and determined that Ridgeons should not be left out. It was certainly the right time, since the DIY industry was still in its infancy and there was as yet little competition.

Ridgeons had already taken one step in this direction. One day in the early 1970s the salesman from Hygena had called on Peter Silk. There was something, he said, he

excellent links with suppliers, who appreciated feedback from customers on how products could be improved. By early 1980 the number of staff had risen to ten, including the first full-time representative, Reg Claringbold, and the number of customer accounts to 230. CRS Wholesale also became the first part of Ridgeons to be linked with the new computer system. In 1983 annual sales exceeded £100,000 for the first time.

David Ridgeon also turned his attention to the firm's plant hire business, which had continued after the Second World War in a small way. He was sure that there was more potential in plant hire, and on the basis that accountants should get to grips with the 'nuts and bolts' of the business, he asked Michael Symons to develop the concept. This led to the creation of Ridgehire, based at Cavendish Road, initially under the management of Dick Dolling. It was anticipated that most customers would be enthusiasts for do-it-yourself

Above: 1970s showroom. Dennis Stanley (now a 25 Club member) began his working life with Ridgeons in this department.

wanted to show him. He produced a flat package and asked Peter Silk to time him. Silk had no idea what he was talking about and watched in amazement as the salesman opened the package and began putting together a kitchen unit. This transformed the way kitchens – and, later, bedrooms – were supplied, and it also enabled a much wider range of stock to be held. Peter Silk was enthusiastic and in 1974 the company opened up a separate department to sell the new units to trade and retail customers. Known as PKB (Packaged Kitchens & Bedrooms), it was based in premises acquired at the Mill Road end of Tenison Road, under the management of Terry Parker. Peter Silk recalled that PKB was so successful that there were queues forming outside as people waited to load up their vans and cars. Terry Parker remembered how they crammed as much as possible into their vehicles, ruining their springs, to benefit from a discount on collection of between 50p and £1 a unit.

Just as PKB was opening, the company was contemplating the closure of its showrooms in Regent Street. It was no longer practical to have an outlet in the centre of Cambridge as the growing volume of traffic precipitated extensive parking restrictions. By the time Dennis Stanley joined Ridgeons at Regent Street in 1975, deliveries were limited to the hours between 7.30 a.m. and 9.30 a.m. on a Tuesday. Instead, the showrooms were moved to a refurbished store at Tenison Road in 1978. When Nick Moss, who started with the company in 1974, joined Dennis Stanley at the new showroom, he found, just as Derrick Brook had, that Tenison Road was still reminiscent of 'a shanty town', a collection of corrugated tin buildings painted in Ridgeon blue by Cyril Upchurch, the maintenance man, whose other standard colour was a pale pink – yet in the middle of them stood this attractive new showroom, with a wonderful wooden staircase handmade by Unwin's, displaying Agas and Rayburns, kitchens and bathrooms. Even 15 years later, an advertisement tried to make a virtue of the unusual location. Headed 'Never Judge A Book By Its Cover', it described how a customer, deterred by a security barrier from heading for Tenison Road to seek out kitchen displays, parked instead at the Octopus store, only then spying the Ridgeons showroom. Making her way towards it through the builders' vans, forklifts and dust of the yard, she found herself transported into a different world found inside the unprepossessing premises. This difficult navigation was not the complete story. Once a customer had ordered an item from the showroom, he or she then either had to drive through the Cambridge traffic down to

A famous visitor to the Tenison Road site, former prime minister John Major.

Cavendish Road to pick it up or else have it delivered. Such inconvenience did not deter one famous customer, John Major, later to become prime minister. About the same time Prince Edward, studying in Cambridge, was a regular visitor to the firm's counters when he was refurbishing a house. When arrangements were being made for his bills to be forwarded to Buckingham Palace, some staff thought at first that their legs were being pulled.

As the number of converts to DIY increased, more and more retail customers passed through the doors of the Cambridge business. This became a problem because long queues of irritated tradesmen regularly formed behind any retail customer whose lack of DIY knowledge demanded much more time and attention from those serving at the counter. To capitalise on the DIY trend, capture more retail customers and alleviate the pressure on trade counters, David Ridgeon planned a purpose-built DIY store, emulating those of the emerging national chains, under a completely new name to mark it out from the merchants' business. This was a confident investment, made possible not only by the improved profitability of the business, but also because Ridgeons was just completing the purchase of the Tenison Road site. This latter accomplishment owed much to Michael Symons. One of his earliest decisions on joining Ridgeons turned out to be one of the most important he made. Checking the company's leases in 1973, he realised that the Tenison Road lease had just ten years to run. Failure to renew the lease would pose a significant threat to the future of the business. Tortuous negotiations began with British Rail to extend the lease. He persuaded British Rail to agree to a new 125-year lease, but this was

granted only on condition that half the site should be developed, a hopelessly impracticable proposition for a builders' merchant. Instead, Symons pursued the purchase of the site, but discussions reached a stalemate, with British Rail refusing to budge. A few years later, with negotiations at an impasse, Symons was filled with indignation when he read in his newspaper that British Rail alleged they lacked any funds for development. He promptly wrote to his MP, pointing out that British Rail was making this claim when it was refusing to sell the land at Tenison Road. Strangely, British Rail suddenly became much more cooperative, an acceptable offer was made by Ridgeons and the company acquired the freehold of the site in 1978.

A year later, the new DIY centre was underway. It was opened on 1 February 1980 under the management of Tony Davis, who had supervised its design and construction. A circular issued in advance of the opening stated that the store 'aims to provide a complete home centre with something of interest for all the family'. Heavy advertising was an integral part of running the new store, which also opened at the weekends. The PKB department was integrated within it. It was just unfortunate that the time lag between planning and completion placed the opening at the start of a serious recession. The new name was unusual, for the store was called the Octopus Home Centre, since the

octopus with its tentacles was thought to be the best image to represent a store stocking so many items. When David Ridgeon told the board, there was a stunned silence, but, as he recounted a few years later, 'Olli grew on us, he's very friendly and so versatile that his tentacles get everywhere!'

This too had valuable lessons for Ridgeons. For the first time, the company had broken away from the traditional way in which building materials had been sold. In the early 1970s, for instance, the paint counter at Tenison Road was no more than 3 or 4 feet (92–122cm) wide, all the goods hidden behind it, and any attempt at display limited to a few dusty items behind glass at the front of the counter. All this changed. Bright, cheerful and welcoming, the Octopus store set an example that helped the company to modernise the

Left: Timber operations at Cavendish Road, c.1970s. Far left is a 48-inch fore cutter, which saws and cuts the untreated wood into planks. Right: The wood is then smoothed and planed in the giant planers. 1980s health and safety regulations required both pieces of machinery to be enclosed within special noise casings to keep the sound to a minimum.

Above: Bill Feakes' retirement party, 1980. From left: John Cook, Bill Feakes, Mrs Feakes and David Ridgeon.

way in which it sold and displayed all goods throughout the business.

One of the remarkable aspects of this period under David Ridgeon's leadership is how many different developments were being carried out simultaneously. Timber operations also came under scrutiny. By the early 1970s the volume of timber sales had been static for a decade, due partly to changes in the trade, with the rise of timber engineering, the decline in demand for second fixings and the use of other materials, such as chipboard. In 1973 David Ridgeon commissioned a report on the future of the timber operations at Cavendish Road from the Timber Research and Development Association (TRADA). This criticised the mill for being out of date, inefficient and having a poor layout. A number of improvements were recommended, including investment in new plant and the appointment of an operations manager. Over the next few years a series of measures were taken to restructure the mill, including measures to meet modern health and safety requirements, such as the enclosure of machines to reduce noise.

In 1980 Bill Feakes retired as director in charge of timber after 50 years with the company. In his place David Ridgeon appointed Alan Newbury, who had joined the company earlier to ease the handover from Bill Feakes. Alan came

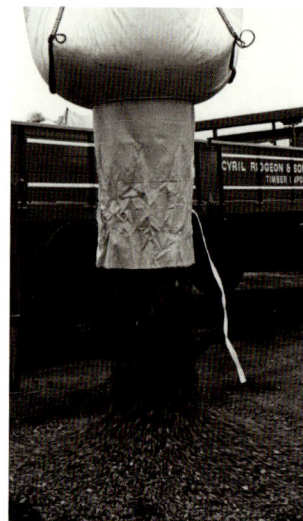

with considerable experience in timber technology, to take charge initially of the Cambridge-based timber operations. There he oversaw further improvements to the Cavendish Road mill, with new planers and moulders, the introduction of rollerways and a rebuilt and modernised toolroom. He was also given the task of working towards the integration of timber operations across Cambridge and Saffron Walden. This was achieved in the early 1980s, allowing Saffron Walden to enjoy the benefits of group purchasing and stocks. In 1981 the company also agreed a franchise with a manufacturer of timber-framed housing to supply packages from Saffron Walden. By then as many as 20 per cent of housing starts in East Anglia were timber-framed, but this venture proved short lived.

Sustained investment in mechanical handling equipment transformed the efficiency of operations and levels of customer service at both Tenison Road and Cavendish Road. Yet the manual handling or handballing of goods was still widespread within the business in the early 1970s. Nigel Haslop remembered the daily delivery of red-hot cement, unloaded by hand into the cement shed, which stood on stilts. This vanished soon after David Ridgeon's arrival, with the erection of a new cement and bag store designed for the operation of forklift trucks. In 1979 a sand bagging plant was set up at Tenison Road, with 1 ton canvas bags with sling handles loaded by cranes onto lorries. Ridgeons was among the first merchants to take up the new method, complying with new weights and measures regulations. Later adopted for smaller bags as well, this proved to be very profitable and was quickly extended to Saffron Walden. To maximise

John Doggett, building materials manager, supervising the sandbagging plant at Tenison Road (top left).

The sand is supplied loose from Dickerson's pit at Waterbeach Quarry before being bagged into 50kg and 1 ton bags.

space on sites that were becoming increasingly cramped as business grew, sliding rack systems, a novel concept at the time, were installed in some branches from the early 1980s.

The advantages of mechanical handling continued to influence the development of the business at Saffron Walden. The boom of the early 1970s had produced acute congestion in Station Street as it became crowded with builders' trucks, and as a result, a new yard and warehouse were opened in 1975. The description of the new development in the local newspaper read:

in place of rapidly deteriorating buildings and an area in which it was chaotic to say the least for lorries and forklift trucks to operate without running into each other, they [the customers] will find a completely redesigned area. Where lorries once found themselves unable to get out of the yard once they were in, there is now space for 15 vehicles to manoeuvre comfortably and to load simultaneously at specially built loading bays.

Fourteen buildings of all shapes and sizes had been demolished to make way for the new warehouse, designed for forklift operations with ramp loading facilities. The opening was used to organise an exhibition in cooperation and this was with major suppliers, attended by more than 1,200 people over two days.

Derrick Brook, appointed an executive director in 1978 with enhanced responsibilities, was working hard to market the company. James Williams, the senior salesman at Saffron Walden, was appointed Group Field Sales Manager in 1979. By this time customers were able to pay for goods with credit cards, not just at Cambridge but also at Saffron Walden, thanks to the initiative of Ken Miller, who joined Ridgeons as company accountant in 1978. The post of advertising manager was created in 1980, when the first holder was Don Harwood, who organised the appearance of five Bond Girls from the latest Bond film, *Octopussy*, for

Bottom left: Aerial view of the Saffron Walden site at Station Street.

Below left: Programme for Ridgeons' trade exhibition, Fiesta.

Below right: Steven Sutton.

Bottom: Front elevation of the site.

the opening of the DIY store. In the same year Derrick Brook organised the company's first major trade exhibition, under the name Fiesta 81, held in marquees at Sawston Hall, just outside Cambridge. Brook later recalled how the owner, initially reluctant, was won over. On the night before the show, just as Brook was retiring to his caravan on the site, exhausted from all the preparation, there was a knock on the door. It was the owner with a bottle of whisky – he finally left with an empty bottle at one in the morning. A huge success, yielding more than £300,000 in orders, the show was repeated the following year, when it was held on Newmarket Racecourse. Under Steve Sutton, Don Harwood's successor, these shows became an annual fixture as part of a wider marketing campaign, which involved fishing days, bowls days, golf days and day trips to France for customers, lunches for the directors of larger client companies and the participation of a Ridgeons team in local charity fun runs.

The gloomy economic situation of the late 1970s and early 1980s did little to hold back the business, which by 1980 was employing 500 staff, turning over more than £20m and making profits in excess of £1m. The only bad news was the closure of the Unwin's joinery business in 1979, but this had nothing to do with the recession. For some years, it had been proving difficult to find continuous work for Unwin's. In an attempt to keep the business open, a small DIY store on the site was planned. However, when planning permission was refused, the business was wound down, finally closing in October 1979 with the loss of 16 jobs. This deeply upset David Ridgeon, for the company had a tradition of never making any employee redundant. The site in Histon High Street was sold for development. Another venture proved short-lived. In 1981 Minimix, the company's own ready-mix concrete supply section, was set up at Tenison Road. A brave attempt to enter a very competitive section of the market, this proved to be a failure. But David Ridgeon was unafraid of making mistakes. As he pointed out a few years later, his aim was to create a group that was 'sufficiently large to be reasonably competitive but [that]

can react quickly to the market place and can introduce new products sooner than some of our larger competitors. We can therefore have a go – some you win, some you lose.' The important thing was making sure that in the final reckoning you had more winners than losers.

With so many developments affecting both Cambridge and Saffron Walden, a group identity began to emerge in the early 1980s. Derrick Brook recalls being asked to advise on the first set of group stationery. Training had been organised on a group basis since the mid-1970s. In March 1982 a conference of managers was held at Churchill College. Paul Rogers, who joined the business in 1979, later becoming an executive director, remembered this as being the first attempt to plan for the future as a group. Although the directors involved with Cambridge and Saffron Walden carried on meeting separately, they began to hold joint meetings as well. Regular meetings for managers and departmental meetings for all staff were also introduced in the early 1980s. With the growth of the business and the need to improve the calibre and foster the development of management, consideration was given to setting up a formal group executive board.

It was at a managers' meeting in the early 1980s that Jimmy Nunn mentioned how some of his recently retired relatives were visited regularly by staff from their former

Ridgeons Fun Run, Sunday, 4 September 1988, Parker's Piece, in the centre of Cambridge with Pat Pagram (centre) leading the way.

Left: Ridgeons' letterheads through the years. Top left: Cyril Ridgeon's original letterhead, dated 1922 in his own handwriting.

Middle left: 1960s stationery. The brown shade in the letterhead was specially chosen to match the brown ink ribbon in the firm's typewriters at the time.

Bottom left: Letterhead from 1980s, incorporating the RIdgeons Group identity.

Below: A summer barbecue at David and Jill Ridgeon's home at Rectory Farm, c.1983. David Ridgeon with Gladys Ridgeon.

Bottom: Firing up the barbecue: 25 Club members Michael Rowell, John Doggett, Ron Coleman and Terry Belcher.

employer. David Ridgeon was taken with this idea, especially as the number of retired staff was steadily increasing. He asked Ivor Warren, who had recently retired, to set up what became the Ridgeon Group LinkScheme in 1982. Seven retired employees were appointed to maintain links with retired staff and take an interest in their care and welfare. This pastoral concern continued to manifest itself among serving staff. From Michael Symons, the idea was adopted of awarding every employee an additional half-day of holiday for every year of service prior to their impending retirement. This helped older staff to wind down their working lives, at the same time allowing the next generation to assume greater responsibilities. Financial advice or assistance with healthcare was made available to staff if they required it. It was a Christian example typical of the family since the days of the founder. In July 1983 the first payments were made from the new group profit-sharing scheme, which had started in September the previous year. Although the heyday of social clubs organised and funded by companies was passing, staff appreciated the opportunities still made available by the company. For instance, in the spring of 1983 a fishing club – which proved very popular – was formed with support from the company. The Ridgewood Fishing Club was based at a properly stocked fishing lake with 3 acres of water at Barway. Members of the 25 Club enjoyed regular summer barbecues at the Rectory Farm, home of David and Jill Ridgeon. An annual Christmas party

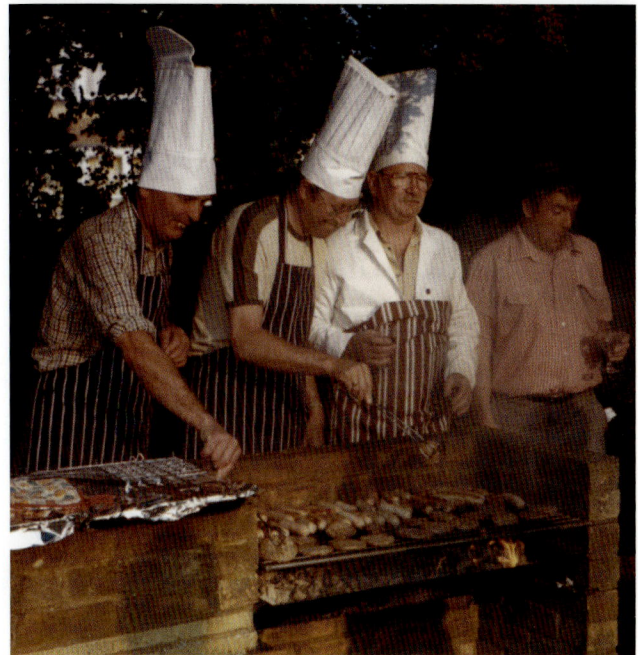

was still organised for some years until the number of employees made it impractical. It was held for a while in the University Centre, spread over several floors, hosting a band, cabaret and disco, with Peter Silk acting as bingo caller. Many employees appreciated the community spirit within the business, which made it feel so welcoming for newcomers. David Ridgeon not only knew everyone by name, he also knew about their families, and, as Gary Stroud recalled, you were 'made to feel part of the family'. At Saffron Walden, Marion Smith and Ann Thomson remembered how staff regularly took part in the local carnival, working through their lunch hours to dress the floats. A team often took part in the carnival bed race. One year the bed was dressed up as a medieval castle with Alan Thompson as a comely maiden, pushed around the town square by four men at high speed.

David Ridgeon had always wanted to set up more branches of the business outside Cambridge. It was a long time since March and Saffron Walden had been acquired. The company was always on the lookout for suitable businesses or sites but they were difficult to find. In 1983 he spotted an advertisement for the sale of a builders' merchant based in Attleborough in Norfolk. This was Allen's Stores (Rocklands) Ltd, operating from a site of about an acre with ten staff. As a country store it stocked an enormous range of goods, including pet food and udder cream, but it was focused on heavy building materials and basic plumbing goods. David Ridgeon paid a visit, recognised the underlying potential of the business and, as he said, 'I thought we should have a go at it'. With an enhanced range of products, it began trading, under manager John Waters, in January 1984, changing its name to Ridgeons in July. Incidentally, this acquisition brought Ridgeons the account of a major customer, Bennett Homes, which it had been courting for some time, thanks to the local representative for Attleborough, Mr Rix.

An issue increasingly pressing by the early 1980s was the future of Ridgeons in Cambridge. It was paramount to maintain Ridgeons as the leading merchant in the city, but both sites were in need of further modernisation and investment. One problem was the fact that the business was split between two sites, to the inconvenience of customers. Another was the growing traffic congestion in Cavendish Road. When a property was purchased in Cromwell Road (at the other end of the site) for the future creation of a much-needed new entrance in 1982, new plans were drawn up. Local residents were becoming increasingly restless about the rising volume of larger lorries queuing outside the Cavendish and Cromwell Road sites, and the acquisition of the freehold of the Tenison Road site gave the group the chance to rethink its future completely. In fact, since the mid-1970s Ridgeons had been looking – without success – at a number of possible new sites in the city. In 1982 the conference at Churchill College raised the idea of a two-site operation in Cambridge, with one site further out of town, both geared to one-stop shopping.

The urgency of the situation was brought home dramatically at the end of 1984. Entertaining managers to Christmas drinks at Rectory Farm on 22 December, David Ridgeon received a telephone call. A major fire had broken out at Cavendish Road. The party was abandoned as everyone made for the site, the glow from the blaze lighting up the night sky. The heat was so intense that it buckled steel structures and turned concrete pink. Local residents in Cromwell Road were evacuated while more than 100 firemen fought the flames. Staff moved timber packs away from the fire as the air was filled with the stench of burning and acrid smoke. On the following day staff worked to

Below: The Cavendish Road branch suffererd a devastating fire on the evening of 22 December 1984. It destroyed 30,000 square feet of timber, the sales office, timber sheds, a lorry, three sideloaders and a forklift truck and caused an estimated £750,000 worth of damage.

Right: David Ridgeon (left) surveys the damage with Alan Newbury (centre) and Peter Silk (right).

Below right: The clean-up operation begins.

organise replacement supplies of timber, plywood and boards to ensure the site could re-open after the Christmas/New Year holiday. Many suppliers willingly gave their assistance. Wives and daughters brought down tea and sandwiches. The fire destroyed more than 800 tons of stacked timber as well as sheds, a lorry and other machinery, causing over £750,000 of damage. The danger posed by the compound of Calor Gas cylinders was exaggerated by the press, for many of the cylinders were empty, they all had a fail-safe device allowing gas to escape rather than explode, and stocks were lower in any case as pre-Christmas deliveries had just been made. The cause of the fire was never identified but arson was strongly suspected. Two or three years later, after another fire in the area, two local adolescents were charged. Although they were then linked to the Ridgeons blaze, there was insufficient evidence to charge them. David Ridgeon remarked that he hoped this would be the only time the company ever appeared under the 'Stop Press' section of the *Sunday Times* front page under those circumstances.

6 The Cambridge Conundrum
1984–97

THE CONUNDRUM OF what to do about Cambridge would dominate discussions about the future of the group throughout the 1980s and 1990s. The improvement in the economy after the early 1980s, fuelled by reductions in direct taxation and the easy availability of cheap credit, helped the group to achieve record turnover and profits by the end of the decade. It was only as the boom evaporated once again that it became clear just how much of a diversion from keeping an eye on the management of the group the future of the Cambridge sites had become. The sadness of dealing with the first serious job losses in the group's history encouraged a determination to resolve the problem once and for all. By 1997 the group could boast two of the largest and most up-to-date branches of any builders' merchant anywhere in the country.

Previous pages: Aerial view of Herringswell mill, a 12-acre timber processing site purchased in 1986.

Above: Front entrance, Ridgeons, Cromwell Road.

The results for 1984 were very positive. As a whole, the group recorded growth of 10 per cent, and the ability of the group to unlock the potential of underperforming locations was apparent from the 24 per cent increase in revenue from the Attleborough branch. With 520 staff, a regular monthly newspaper, the *Ridgeon Recorder*, was introduced to improve communications within a much more dispersed and varied business.

During the year serious investigations began into the possibility of redeveloping the Cambridge business on the site of the former Blue Circle cement works in Coldhams Lane. This came with the huge disadvantage that it had been used since closure as a landfill site for refuse. The land was still settling and there was the hazard of methane gas to contend with. Yet it had taken over two years to find even this site with all its disadvantages. To overcome the problem of land settlement, Ridgeons seriously considered the possibility of erecting buildings on stilts on the site. Consultants were employed and a great deal of time and effort was invested in the assessment of the site. When the report was received in the spring of 1984, David Ridgeon told his directors it showed that 'the proposal for a "new" greenfield site' wasn't on. He felt they should 'pursue the development of our two existing complexes'. But opinion on the matter was fluid. At the end of the same directors' meeting in March 1984, the minutes concluded that 'we almost talked ourselves back into a one-stop greenfield new development'. A few months later the Coldhams Lane proposal was finally abandoned, killed off by the prohibitive costs of development, estimated at £11m, and the risk of methane gas. Redeveloping the existing Cavendish Road site was also dismissed at the time, since the costs of £9m for the proposed scheme seemed unaffordable.

Above: Copies of the *Ridgeon Recorder*, which was started in 1984.

Below left: Putting together an early issue of the magazine.

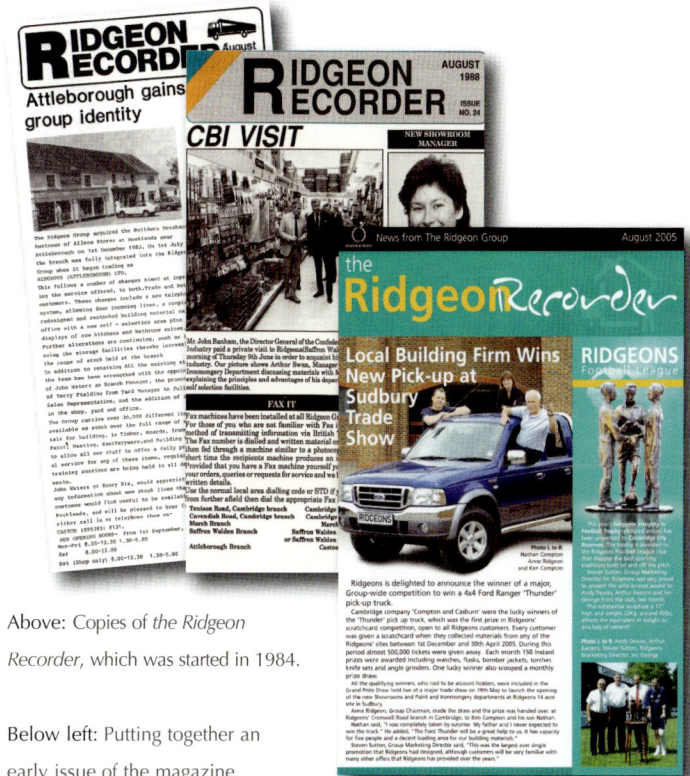

While this was going on, the Saffron Walden business was undergoing its biggest change since its acquisition by Ridgeons in 1958. It had been planned to redevelop the firm's existing location in Station Street, but, as Peter Lawrence wisely pointed out, this would do nothing to improve either the security of the site or its poor location. Whatever was done, some vehicles would have to continue unloading on the roadside, while it would be difficult to operate the site without maintaining the multiple access points that made security so difficult. Lawrence suggested that the board should visit the extensive 32-acre site on the edge of town recently vacated by the engineering firm Acrow, which had been taken into receivership. The main building on the site covered some 100,000 square feet, divided internally by a central roadway. James Williams remembered that although David Ridgeon had said he wanted to find a bigger location, Williams never thought he would take on such a large site. For David Ridgeon, on the other hand, the potential of the site was obvious. Shortly after the visit, made in December 1984, Ridgeons made an offer acceptable to the receiver. Buying property when prices were depressed proved to be characteristic of the group, a shrewd approach mirrored by selling when prices were high. David Ridgeon's vision of the development was innovative, based on making it as straightforward as possible for the customer to do business, with easy access, plenty of storage space and parking, and all products under one roof. For good communications between departments, a post tube system was installed. James Williams, deeply involved in executing the project, recalled the many planning hurdles that had to be overcome, for the planners had exercised caution, since it was believed there was no precedent for a similar development on such a scale anywhere in the United States or Europe. The project management firm appointed by the group, Wilby & Burnett, did a great job, and the task was undertaken and completed by the successful contractors, Duncan Cameron & Hutchinson Ltd of Braintree. To satisfy the planners, the existing sawmill at Shirehill was closed at the same time and a new one set up in another suitable building.

The move from Station Street to Ashdon Road was phased over nine weeks. Even so, Ann Thomson, who joined as a receptionist in 1973, remembered how the reception area was incomplete when the move took place. Since it was still being built around her, the builders had to help her up and over the counter whenever she had her tea break, and the receptionists had to hold up their hands to silence the drills

Below left: Saffron Walden's new site at Ashdon Road, 1987. Director Derrick Brook (left) and David Ridgeon (second from right) with visitors.

Bottom: The Ashdon Road premises were opened by Lord Skelmersdale (pictured third from right). From left: James Williams, Terry Wilby, Michael Baynes (of Forum Architects) David Gandy

(former President BMF), Alan Hazelhurst MP, Lord Skelmersdale (Minister), Derrick Brook and David Ridgeon.

Below: Touring the site. From left: Lord Skelmersdale, David Ridgeon, Alan Hazelhurst, Toni Gandy, David Gandy, Paul Rogers, Peter Gill (Director BMF) and Steven Sutton.

when they took a phone call. The only disadvantage of the move, as Eddie Izard remembered, was that it was no longer possible, as it had been at Station Street, to nip out for a bag of chips or a swift haircut. Making use of the existing central roadway, the undercover drive-through system was opened in 1987 by Lord Skelmersdale, the Parliamentary Under Secretary at the Department of the Environment. Once the site was up and running, its innovative operation attracted regular visitors from home and abroad. Each day more than 200 staff served over 700 customers, generating sales in excess of £15m a year, a far cry from the 20 staff employed a generation earlier. One member of staff who did not make the move was Les Camp, who retired shortly beforehand,

Above: Les Camp retired after 50 years' service at Ridgeons, mostly based at Saffron Walden. From left: David Ridgeon, a Ridgeons customer, Les Camp with his retirement gifts, Albert Ridgwell and Graham Shand.

Above right: Alan Thompson receiving his 25 Club gift from Mrs Joan Ridgeon.

Left: Gordon Ridgeon.

Below left: The new Group logo.

Below: Rachel Anderson (née Ridgeon).

having served 50 years at Saffron Walden. Alan Thompson, who retired in the year the Ashdon Road site was purchased, pinpointed one of the principal reasons for the firm's success in his leaving speech. His remarks could apply equally well to the whole group: 'for if anything makes success, it is caring. Caring that customers are given good service, that they get what they want when they want, being courteous and helpful, caring that the information customers are given is correct and up to date.'

This major step forward for the whole business was accompanied by the decision at last to integrate the Saffron Walden business within the group under the Ridgeons name. It had been decided at the end of 1985 that all businesses associated with the group would trade as Ridgeons. Bringing Saffron Walden into the group also had the advantage of creating a single board of executive directors. Steve Sutton, prior to becoming Marketing Director, devised a new logo combining the gold from Saffron Walden's previous logo with the Ridgeons blue. By the end of 1992 the group identity had been further rationalised, so that Ridgeons (Saffron Walden), Ridgeons (March) and Ridgeons (Attleborough) simply became Ridgeons.

David Ridgeon was taking steps to strengthen the group's management. All this simultaneous activity had placed considerable strain on the group's senior executives. In addition, Alan Thompson retired in 1985, and Peter Silk was

intending to step down in 1987. Derrick Brook became director in charge of Saffron Walden, with the purpose of supporting and developing other managers, while two new executive directors, Terry Parker and Paul Rogers, were appointed. These moves reflected David Ridgeon's constant concern to develop management at all levels within the group and ensure continuity and succession.

At the same time, younger members of the family were joining the business. Michael Ridgeon's son, Gordon, came to the group in 1985 after gaining experience with Sharp & Fisher and the Graham Group. David's daughter, Rachel, came with experience in law and accountancy and spent over three years working for the group before her marriage in May 1992, having become a non-executive director a few months previously.

Powermat 2000

This page: Herringswell Timber Mill, 2008 (above), shown here operated by Adrian Hayes (top). Kerry Golding stacks the sorted pieces of timber (far right). The mill revolutionalised the production and processing of timber for Ridgeons and made Herringswell one of the top production units in the country.

Below right: Mill operators at Herringswell today.

Facing page: The latest extractor plant that recycles hot air to keep the mill at a constant temperature.

all group outlets. The review concluded that a major central production unit, including a new mill and treatment plants, should be established on a new site. This would also take the place of the small mill operated at Saffron Walden. Newmarket, with easier access and a better labour market, was chosen as the preferred area. The journey time from Newmarket to Cambridge was exactly the same as that for deliveries made within Cambridge from Cavendish Road. But suitable alternatives rarely came on the market or, if they did, were snapped up quickly, since other operators had similar problems. When an 11-acre site appeared for sale in the summer of 1986 the group quickly submitted an offer – swift decision-making was one advantage of being a private family business – and plans were made for the new development. This would precipitate the redevelopment of Cavendish Road, funded by the sale of Tenison Road.

As it turned out, negotiations were protracted and contracts had still not been exchanged by early December, when a better opportunity came up. The 12-acre site at Herringswell, near Newmarket, came on the market because, like the previous occupants of Ashdon Road, its operators, the Eastern Counties Timber Group, had been taken into receivership. Since it was an existing timber yard,

While the Ashdon Road project was underway, the group's timber operations were undergoing an equally significant change. When Alan Newbury was appointed as group executive in charge of timber in 1985 he carried out a review of the business. The problems of operating a central Cambridge location were becoming increasingly difficult, and it was clearly desirable to move the timber business out of the city. First, it would release more space for the expansion of other activities at Cavendish Road, and second, it would allow the centralisation of bulk handling and the processing of timber and boards for distribution to it could be up and running very quickly, and it would be much less expensive to adapt. Eastern Counties collapsed on 20 November, David Ridgeon became aware of the site on 9 December, the directors discussed the acquisition on 18 December, an offer of £600,000 was made to the receiver (Mark Palios, later briefly chief executive of the Football Association) on 23 December, and the deal was completed on New Year's Eve. The advantage of wrapping things up so quickly was demonstrated early in the New Year. David Ridgeon was at Herringswell when another interested party arrived, assuming the site was still available. It turned out they were from the group's major rivals, Travis Perkins, and it gave David Ridgeon great satisfaction to let them know they were too late.

By the spring of 1987 Herringswell was supplying all the planed and moulded timber for every outlet in the group. Alan Newbury, with Mike Cammack, had been instrumental in planning the new mill, managed by Paul Mazey. A stress-grading machine was added, together with additional sorting facilities to the moulding line to eliminate handling and permit the processing of carcassing to customer specifications as well as joinery timber. The new processing line, overseen by Kerry Golding and costing in excess of half a million pounds, allowed for the first time the production of a complete range of pre-graded planed and regularised timber, with a choice of over a hundred different mouldings. Once again, training was an important component of the new venture. Key personnel had been sent on courses with Weinig, the machinery manufacturer in Germany, and on-site training had also been carried out.

The group training scheme had been introduced in 1985, giving trainees the opportunity to spend time in several departments over two years, improving their knowledge of general building materials for the benefit of customers. The Ridgeons Advanced Training Scheme (RATS) was the idea of Terry Parker, aimed at management trainees. One such trainee was Bob Butler, who later became the group's purchasing executive. As part of the course participants spent a week on a team-building exercise at the Outward Bound Centre in Eskdale. Gary Stroud, who joined the group in 1975, attended the first such week in late 1988, just as the first snow of the winter appeared. Having spent a night under plastic, the trainees awoke to pouring rain. They walked up Scafell Pike, the highest peak in England, pitching their tents in gale force winds, and then faced more than an inch (3cm) of snow the next morning. Staff members were also encouraged to take up business studies, and Terry

Parker was among those who lectured Gary Stroud and others at college. The strength of the group's training was recognised in 1990 when it received the Innovation in Training Award for the most progressive and informative training programme. This was also the year when the group introduced another initiative of Terry Parker's, the Total Customer Care Training Package. Training was always on the agenda for directors' meetings, and occasionally entire meetings were devoted to the subject.

The group, which celebrated its 75th anniversary in 1986, continued to appreciate the service given by staff, past and present. When the annual dinner of the 25 Club was held in 1985, those attending had a combined service of more than 3,400 years. The LinkScheme was still working well and outings were usually organised every year for retired staff that were interested. The Ridgeons Travel Club, ably organised by Jenny Corden, was formed around this time, and excursions arranged during 1987–8 included the Ideal Home Exhibition and the Munich Beer Festival as well as visits to Amsterdam and Paris. The Sports and Social Club was set up during 1988, the idea of Dave Scarrow, and its first event was a charity football match at Histon, featuring an Emlyn Hughes invitation side. Teams throughout the group played sports, from football at Saffron Walden to bowls at March, while inter-branch darts matches were organised by Ernie Francis.

The removal of timber from Cavendish Road released almost 5 acres of land for other uses. More space was freed through relinquishing the Calor Gas franchise. In 1987 this led to another review of the future of the Cambridge business. This time directors concluded that the best option lay in creating a one-stop shopping operation at Cavendish Road, based on a second access from Cromwell Road, funded partly by the sale of Tenison Road. It was also suggested that the redeveloped site should be renamed Cromwell Road to move away from the adverse reputation that all the problems of congestion had brought to the Cavendish Road site.

With so much going on, it is perhaps unsurprising that the only new branch opened by the group until the early 1990s was a second depot for CRS Wholesale. This opened at Rushden in Northamptonshire in 1988 as the wholesale distribution business expanded through the late 1980s boom. But improvements were made at both Attleborough and March. More land was acquired at Attleborough in 1989, where a new warehouse, office and showroom block were added. The March branch was relocated from Creek Road, which was sold, and rebuilt on a 6-acre greenfield site at Martin Avenue on the March Trading Park at Hostmoor. It also included a second Octopus DIY centre and a small timber mill. It had been suggested that the 20,000-square foot Cambridge store should be expanded, but the continuing saga of the Cambridge redevelopment, along with all the other projects underway, persuaded the directors to erect a second smaller store elsewhere.

Above left: Ridgeons celebrated its 75th anniversary in style, with a dinner at King's College, Cambridge, 1986. Editorial features and advertisements were taken out in the local press and the event was emblazoned upon a double-decker bus, which was commissioned specially for the event (above).

Left: David Ridgeon and fellow directors toast the company's success outside the bus.

Above: A second Octopus branch was opened in January 1990, in March, north Cambridgeshire.

Below right: Ridgeons branch at Attleborough.

When the second Octopus opened, along with the new March branch, in January 1990 overall trading conditions had worsened dramatically. Falling tax and interest rates had overheated the economy. A manufacturing base that had contracted badly in the early 1980s was unable to meet the increased demand for consumer goods. Instead these were sucked in from abroad, creating a record balance of payments deficit. House prices soared, inflation reached 10 per cent and interest rates rose to 15 per cent in 1989–90. In the early 1990s it was construction that suffered worst, enduring a recession deeper and longer than expected.

Ridgeons, preoccupied with so much else, was unprepared for this. Turnover had reached £62m (worth £125m today) in 1988, accompanied by record profits of nearly £4m, but then decreased every year, dropping to £47m in 1992. The group was just about breaking even, as profits dipped below a million pounds for three years in a row. Sales fell for 45 months in a row between May 1989 and February 1993. The downturn began slowly in the spring of 1989, as some building sites closed, and worsened steadily throughout the year. In 1990, when Roger Day was urging sales representatives to bring back four orders every day, Gordon Ridgeon remembered that it was a challenge to secure even four orders a week. Michael Symons was cautious, taking action, assisted by Ken Miller, to reduce the group's borrowings by almost half over the next three to four years. A prudent approach at a time of rising interest rates and falling sales, this also ensured the group was in a position to support the future costs of any Cambridge redevelopment. At first, reductions in costs were made in areas that did not involve job cuts. Even as these savings

were met, trade continued to worsen, and Ridgeons watched as some competitors, despite cutting back on staff, went out of business. With the need to save another million pounds, of which 70 per cent had to come from staffing, mainly in administration, the group could not wait any longer if it was to afford the costs that came with redundancies.

For the first time in its history Ridgeons was forced to make a significant number of people redundant. For David Ridgeon, who at the time was president of the Builders' Merchants Federation, it was heartbreaking. He aged visibly in a matter of weeks. His brother Michael remembered how 'it made him really quite ill, you could see he was drained, it hurt him'. In all, 45 jobs went, of which 25 were compulsory redundancies. In October 1990 David Ridgeon wrote, 'It is a very sad day for me when I have to write about losing staff … but now we have no choice.' He described how he and his fellow directors had spent many hours working out a programme of cost reductions that were both fair and right for the group so it could return to profit. Among the other casualties was the Gayhomes hardware store in Saffron Walden. After an offer from Eaden Lilley to rent the premises was accepted, the store closed its doors in May 1990. As Ridgeons fought back, reducing borrowings by more than 20 per cent during 1991, it also gained market share from

rivals, who were faring even worse. More job losses came in 1992. By the time sales began rising once more in 1993, overall staff numbers had been cut by 22 per cent. For Tony Davis the recession was 'the worst time for me in my whole career'; telling people they were losing their jobs was 'extremely unpleasant'. Derrick Brook, who was responsible for implementing job losses at Saffron Walden, was another among many who shared the same feelings. Marion Smith, working at Saffron Walden, where she was responsible for filling out the redundancy payslips, remembered it was 'very traumatic'. 'None of you knew who was going to be next.'

Among those with outstanding service who retired at this time was Mick Rowell, who had been with the group since 1942, spending most of his time at Cavendish Road, where he became yard manager. Jack Anderson had joined Tenison Road as a boy in 1945, eventually working in the mill. Gerald Smith, who came to Ridgeons as an office boy in 1944, became wages clerk and spent almost his entire career in the accounts office. Terry Parker, who had been with the group since 1965, was headhunted to become chief executive of a national heating and sanitaryware distribution business, leaving the group in 1992. He returned five years later to become managing director.

The group took the opportunity to plan coherently for the future. In late 1991 Alan Newbury carried out detailed research into trends for Cambridge. At a special conference held at Blakeney in January 1992, Michael Symons had introduced a leading occupational psychologist, Dr Jean Hammond, who led the directors through the various ways of planning for the future. For James Williams, among others, this heralded a major shift in the group's thinking. It would lead to widening the responsibility for taking major decisions, selecting the right people for the right roles and creating small teams to work together to tackle specific

Left: Mick Rowell, retired in 1992 after 50 years' service.

Below left: Group directors, 1990. Standing from left: Alan Newbury, James Williams, Michael Symons, Ian Forbes and Peter Lawrence. Seated: Tony Davis, Terry Parker, David Ridgeon, Derrick Brook and Paul Rogers.

areas. This began at the conference, which yielded so many ideas that a series of steering groups were formed for each area, and it also improved understanding among directors. Further work on the plan resulted in the announcement later in the year of the Group Philosophy and Company Goals, led and coordinated by Rachel Ridgeon and Paul Rogers. Eight goals were listed, based on customer service, site development, individual development, systems and technology, community and social activities, initiative and responsibility, investment and growth in market share. Resolving the long-running saga about what to do with Tenison Road and Cavendish Road was reaffirmed as the main priority, followed by the need to update the group's computer systems.

It was perhaps the results of the conference that gave David Ridgeon the confidence to announce in 1993 that he was handing over the position of managing director to Michael Symons, the first non-family member to hold the post, while remaining group executive chairman. Like David Ridgeon, Michael Symons believed strongly that the group's most important asset was its people. On his appointment he made the point of spending an hour with every manager, meeting every employee and being introduced regularly to all new staff.

The two key objectives for the group would be achieved almost simultaneously, crowding investment planned for five years into two. But the opportunistic approach to expansion continued – it depended, David Ridgeon would later remark, 'on how the spirit moved'. Identifying new branches remained difficult, but David Ridgeon was keen to make sure the group was prepared to seize appropriate opportunities as they arose. Derrick Brook and James Williams had already been involved in listing priority areas

for new branches. With everything else that was going on it is not surprising that only one new branch was opened. The managing director of SPR Hancock Ltd, a builders' merchant based at Sawbridgeworth, between Bishop's Stortford and Harlow, contacted David Ridgeon early in 1993 to enquire whether he would be interested in taking over the business. David Ridgeon declined, realising that the business was in trouble. When it quickly collapsed, an offer was once again made to the receiver for the property and trading assets. Various planning irregularities were cleared up, considerable work was done to make the buildings sound, and the group's sixth branch opened for business in July that year.

Two years later every branch was benefiting from the new, fully integrated computer system developed by Kerridge Computer Systems, covering accounts, stock, sales and purchasing, and timber processing. It enabled the introduction of bar codes and the transmission of quotations directly to customers via their fax machines. Vivien Storey, who had been with the group since 1980, working on the installation of the original computer system, played a key role in this work. She would retire as group IT manager in 2006.

As ever, work was continuing on the Cambridge project. The idea was once more to develop two sites, one either side of the river, based on Cromwell Road to the south and a new site to the north. This followed research showing that the river was a definite boundary for customers. Sites that met all the necessary planning requirements were not easy to find. Michael Symons made a determined search, which proved fruitful when he spotted an advertisement for a joinery factory at Nuffield Road, off Milton Road, close to the A14. He paid a visit and realised that adjacent units and vacant plots could be combined to create an overall site totalling 5 acres. The location was ideally situated for the delivery of heavy goods, which could be organised on behalf of customers from Cromwell Road through the new computer system. The city council was favourably inclined towards development, and the group eventually concluded

ensuring the group remained competitive. In general, heavy side goods would be concentrated at Nuffield Road, which would be used mainly for delivering building materials, timber, sheet materials, paint and ironmongery direct to customers, although collection would be possible. Cromwell Road, focusing on the light side, was planned for the collection of a similar range of stock, plus sanitaryware and heating goods, adopting a system similar to the one that had been pioneered with such success at Ashdon Road. It would include a new and extensive showroom and remain the location for Ridgehire. The hire department under Ron Bentley, assisted by Peter Sievewright, had been expanded through the acquisition in 1989 of the power tool section of Cambridge Battery Service. The Octopus store would remain at Tenison Road, but the remainder of the site would be sold.

In the meantime, a steering group led by Paul Rogers, with Tony Greavett working full time, had already been working on the details of the project. Consultation was carried out with staff and customers. Lengthy negotiations with the planning authorities for both locations commenced

Above: Tenison Road's final customers, Dr and Mrs Fraser were treated to a bottle of champagne.

Right: The end of an era – the demolition of Tenison Road site, 1991.

Facing page: The new site at Cromwell Road in development.

Planning, development and construction of the site took place over a period of five years. The site was formerly entered via Cavendish Road, but what was the back of the original building was turned around and relaid so that the new site was accessed via Cromwell Road.

negotiations for the fifth of five parcels of land on the site at the end of 1993. The city council insisted on a planning agreement to ensure that the company (excluding Octopus) vacated the Tenison Road premises. After ten years, the searching was over.

The group finally announced its ambitious redevelopment plans for Nuffield Road and Cromwell Road in February 1994. Instead of the previous plans for centralising operations at Cromwell Road, which had been estimated to cost more than £9m, the two sites together were expected to cost £4m. David Ridgeon wrote to every customer, highlighting the objectives of the scheme – making most materials for any job available from either site, except heating and sanitaryware; reducing traffic congestion; and during 1993. Full planning consent was achieved only in April 1995, subject to the allocation of part of the Tenison Road site for low-cost housing.

The winning tender for Nuffield Road came within the budget for the project, and work began on site in February 1995. The development was completed in August, and the site opened as planned on 30 October 1995, offering 50,000 square feet of warehousing.

Things were not as straightforward at Cromwell Road. Dealing with contamination on the site was a problem. Although it was agreed there was no need to remove surface material contaminated as a result of timber treatment, since an impermeable paving was placed over it, a second contaminated area was discovered. Sorting this out resulted in lengthy delays and significant additional costs, with the contaminated soiled having to be transported to Corby. At one point this seemed likely to threaten the viability of the project, but the work was re-phased, costs contained and most of the delays made up. The group made sure that all interested parties, including staff, customers and residents, were kept informed as work continued. Residents received vouchers from the group to say 'thank you' for their forbearance. The first phase, covering CRS Wholesale and the heating and sanitaryware buildings, was finished on time and within budget, and opened gradually between July and September 1995. Work began on the second phase in July 1995, and the completed site began trading on 11 November 1996. At the same time Tenison Road closed after 83 years. A clearance sale was held over two days when a large quantity of old stock was sold off. For Tony Greavett, who joined Ridgeons in 1973 and had been part of the team that implemented the Cambridge redevelopment, the sale 'took you back to your trading days'. In 1997 the land was sold for housing development for £1.5m.

Gordon Ridgeon made a film diary of the work involved at Nuffield Road and later Cromwell Road. Twice a week for nearly two years he would trudge through mud, rubble and paint pots with his video camera. Editing hours of footage, he compiled two five-minute films about each development, which were copied and given to many suppliers and all contractors to thank them all for their part in this major contribution to the company's development.

As the Nuffield Road project moved towards its conclusion, the only downside was that once again it absorbed so much of everyone's time and effort that it proved a distraction from the day-to-day management of the group. This was aggravated by the fact that this coincided with a dip in the economy. The group was also undergoing several changes in senior management. Peter Lawrence, Derrick Brook and Tony Davis, who had each played a key role within the business for so long, all retired between May 1995 and January 1996.

In late 1994 Anne Ridgeon, the younger daughter of David Ridgeon, joined the group. Like her sister, she had graduated from Durham University. She came from a successful career with Saatchi & Saatchi, requesting only that she be given time beforehand to carry out an MBA, which featured a dissertation on the trade. She gradually took over responsibility for marketing, human resources and CRS Wholesale. She had always been very conscious of the importance of the business in family life. Although it was little discussed at home, it was a central part of her own life, through business functions, branch openings and frequent visits to Saffron Walden when her father was working there. She would decide a few years later to take time away from the group, acting as project director for a homeless project in south London. Anne's departure in 1997 was agreed on condition that she would return and take over from her father as chairman. Another change came in 1996 when Alan Pealling was recruited as finance director, taking over some of Michael Symons's responsibilities.

Although Ridgeons emerged without the loss of any jobs, unlike a number of rivals, the group's trading results for 1996 were disappointing, as net profits halved, coming close to the figures recorded during the nadir of the early 1990s. It was a lesson taken to heart. With overheads

Left: Cromwell Road, 2010.

Right: Ridgeons Group Chairman and Cyril Ridgeon's great-granddaughter, Anne Ridgeon.

The official opening of the new Cromwell Road site by HRH the Duke of Edinburgh, 7 July 1997.

Clockwise from top left: His Royal Highness greets David Ridgeon on his arrival at Cromwell Road; David Ridgeon accompanies the Duke on a tour of the site; Inside, His Royal Highness gets to grips with one of the showers on display in the Ridgeons Heating and Sanitaryware department as the managing director Michael Symons looks on; Unveiling the plaque; His Royal Highness sits around the table with senior Ridgeons staff, including Roger Day (second from left); After the tour, the Duke was presented with a gift – a new drill set – by David Ridgeon.

Ridgeons makes its delivery of guttering to the
Royal Estate at Sandringham.

reviewed and reporting systems improved, results for the following year achieved a trebling of net profits. Although this still placed the group behind major rivals, it was a step in the right direction, and the figures showed how the group's performance in Cambridge was already benefiting from the new developments.

On 7 July 1997 Cromwell Road was officially opened by HRH the Duke of Edinburgh, who toured the site, meeting managers and staff. He also ordered several lengths of Osma plastic guttering for marking out his carriage-driving course at Sandringham. While walking around the site, he asked one unsuspecting couple if they had found what they were looking for. They replied politely that they had – but recognised the Duke only when prompted by a nervous manager. The Duke's visit was much appreciated and David Ridgeon was particularly grateful to the Lord Lieutenant for suggesting it in the first place.

The group used the occasion to raise awareness of the Ridgeons name and maintain its leading position in the local market. Two special family days were held to attract customers, with a free barbecue, special offers and demonstrations. A huge trade show was also held for trade customers. Throughout these special events, the emphasis was on the group's key strengths, the expertise of staff and the range and depth of stock.

Cromwell Road boasted 90,000 square feet of warehousing and showroom space, making it one of the largest builders' merchants' sites in the country. Accessibility was the key characteristic of the modern layout, whether it was timber stored in the open or other products reached by covered driveways, making loading simple for customers. At both the new Cambridge branches, formally known as Cambridge North and Cambridge South respectively, counter service was retained, for customers still relied on the knowledge and assistance of Ridgeons staff, but most stock was available on open shelves. At Cromwell Road a proper balance was also achieved between the needs of the public and those of trade customers, who were both able to enjoy the magnificent new showrooms designed and managed by John Dicken.

The completion of Nuffield Road and Cromwell Road was a momentous event in the history of the group. It had taxed the minds of many people for a very long time, but it had given Ridgeons two of the most modern builders' merchants' branches and cemented the group's leading position not just in Cambridge but also in the whole region. To say 'thank you', David and Jill Ridgeon gave a party at their home for all those who had helped in some way, each of them presented with an engraved glass paperweight as a small memento of achieving such an enormous task.

Ridgeons Branches, 2010

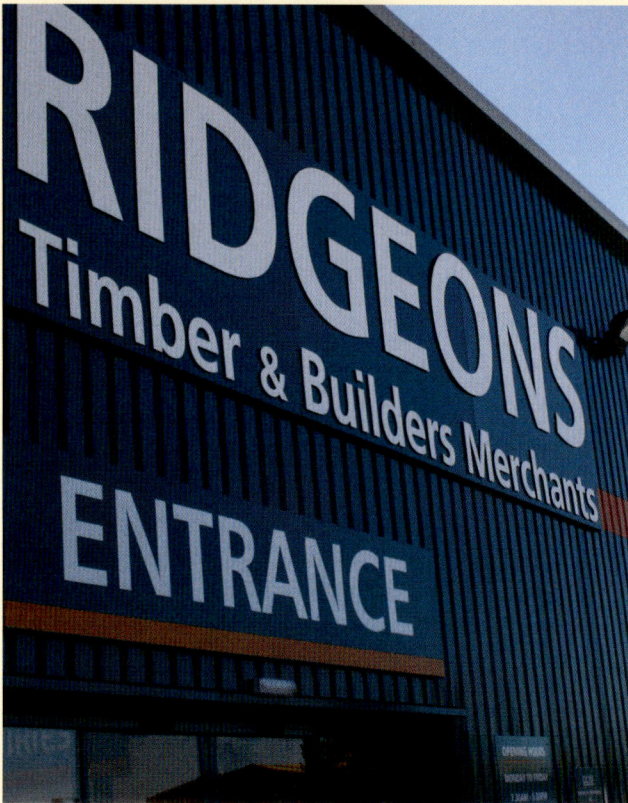

From humble beginnings, the Ridgeon Group has grown to become East Anglia's leading builders' merchant. This page and opposite chart the 100-year journey from the back bedroom of Cyril Ridgeon's home in St Barnabas Road to 22 branches in 2010.

1911 Ridgeons founded by Cyril Ridgeon, St Barnabas Road.

1925 Tenison Road site purchased. Cyril's son Elliot joined the business, which was subsequently renamed Cyril Ridgeon & Son.

1928 Cavendish Road was acquired and a new sawmill was built.

1946 March. A new branch was opened in Broad Street.

1948 Creek Road yard was purchased for building materials, timber, boards, heating and plumbing products. Front of building shows mosaic tile lorry motif (1).

1958 Saffron Walden Building Materials Supply Co. Ltd was bought on Station Road.

1983 Attleborough.

1985 Saffron Walden, a new 32-acre site at Ashdon Road, purchased, moving trade from Station Road in 1986. The branch started trading in August of the following year from 8.5 acres, with almost 2.5 acres all under one roof.

1986 Ridgeons Forest Products (Herringswell), one of the most modern timber production units in the country.

1988 Attleborough. Purchased 1.6 acres of land.

Purchased greenfield site on March Trading Park, 2 miles from the town centre. The new March branch opened January 1990 in 3.9 acres.

1993 Sawbridgeworth (2).

1994 Cambridge Nuffield Road was acquired and opened for business in 1995. A central sales office was officially opened in 1996.

1996 Cambridge Cromwell Road opened.

1998 Snettisham (4).

1999 Halesworth, Ipswich (5), Colchester (6), Newmarket, Thetford, Kelvedon (8).

2001 Bury St Edmunds (9).

2003 Sudbury, Norwich (10), Diss (11), Lowestoft.

2004 Anne Ridgeon became chairman.

2005 Newmarket (7) and Halesworth (12) branches moved to new, larger premises.

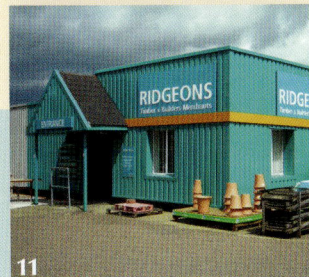

Saffron Walden kitchen and bathroom showrooms and paint and ironmongery department underwent major refurbishments (3).

2006 Anglia Tool Centre, Bury St Edmunds (13).

2007 Pampisford (14).

2007 Peterborough.

2008 Ridgeons Independent Living Centre (15).

2010 Martlesham branch (16).

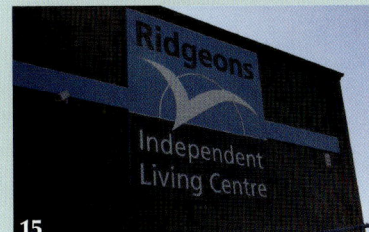

'The Fabric of our Family'
1997 Onwards

7

IN 1997 THE RIDGEONS GROUP was trading from six branches, including two of the largest sites in the UK industry, running a major timber operation and an expanding wholesale business, turning over £65m and employing 680 staff. It was an impressive achievement, providing firm foundations for the expansion that would take place during the next decade.

During 1997 Michael Symons reached 50 and, as he had always said he would, stepped down as managing director while remaining a non-executive director. There had been suggestions that Anne Ridgeon would take up the post, but she insisted that the business required a leader with much deeper experience. That individual was

Terry Parker. On 1 January 1998 he came back to the business after an absence of more than five years as the chief executive of a major business in the industry, which he had returned to profit.

Previous pages: Managers' conference at the Newmarket Racecourse, 2006.

Facing page: Staff in the timber store, 2010.

Above: Directors mark the further expansion of Ridgeons across East Anglia with the acquisition of six new branches from Marlows, 1998. From left: Alan Newbury, Paul Rogers, David Ridgeon, Alan Pealling, Terry Parker and Rachel Anderson.

Above: Staff recipients of long-service awards at Cromwell Road, 2010.

Below right: Members of the 25 Club, 2008.

With an expanding workforce, Gordon Ridgeon suggested the idea of reviving the long-service awards for staff, which had long since ceased to exist. The first awards were made in 1998, and the new scheme dovetailed with the admission of long-serving staff into the 25 Club. For several years ceremonies were held at various venues around the region until they were amalgamated into two large events held in Cambridge. They have since been complemented by another award celebrating 25 years of employment, which takes into account the period of time served by staff in businesses acquired by Ridgeons. In addition, members of the 25 Club who achieve 35 years of service receive a further award at the club's annual dinner.

Within two years the group more than doubled its number of branches from six to 14. The first addition came on 1 October 1998 with James Lambert & Sons Ltd, an established Norfolk firm that had been trading from Snettisham, between King's Lynn and Hunstanton, since the late 18th century but whose owner had no successors. The acquisition followed the pattern set at Sawbridgeworth. The group acquired the assets of the business, which included

He was well regarded, he knew the group and many of its staff and, most importantly, he shared its values. He took the view, with which David Ridgeon and his fellow directors agreed, that the business should aim to achieve a turnover of £100m within ten years to secure its leading regional position against fierce competition from national chains. The latter were growing rapidly, particularly through the acquisition of smaller independent merchants, and the industry was undergoing a sustained period of consolidation. Expansion was the surest way to make sure Ridgeons flourished and continued to give employment to so many families.

To achieve this goal, the business embarked on a conscious programme of branch expansion. The group identified gaps in its coverage of the region and sought to fill them, either by identifying businesses for acquisition or by setting up completely new branches. Terry Parker asked Tony Greavett to undertake the task. For six months he travelled all over East Anglia, armed with a camera, clipboard and high-visibility vest. It was surprising how this uniform usually persuaded people to accept that he was entitled to be wandering around. He inspected every builders' merchant and every showroom, gathering information during the day and writing up his notes every evening. These were contained in volumes covering each county. For instance, the one for Essex ran to 155 pages, consisting of a brief description of every merchant, with photographs, together with location maps and details of the population density of each settlement or area.

three good warehouses and a paint and ironmongery building on a site of one acre, and over several weeks it was transformed into a Ridgeons branch. Tony Greavett – who had been the link between Ridgeons and James Lambert, the owner – supervised the work. It would prove to be a huge success. In 2005 Ridgeons at Snettisham successfully re-applied to hold the royal warrant for supplying materials to the Sandringham estate. In the same year its dynamic young manager, Neil Kimber, became branch manager of the year under the Builders' Merchant Awards for Excellence. Like Sawbridgeworth, it was run as a satellite of the March branch under John Mortlock.

Soon afterwards, on 31 March 1999, came the second acquisition in this series. This was another existing business, that of J.E. Mellon & Sons Ltd in Kelvedon, lying to the west of Colchester. Tony Greavett again took charge of converting the branch and Nigel Haslop acted as the interim manager.

On 1 October 1999 six branches were bought from the well-established business of Marlows, for which Derrick Brook had once worked. When the owner approached David Ridgeon about the possibility, he naturally enquired why he had come to Ridgeons. It was, the owner said, because his staff had asked him to do so, a sign of the respect in which the group was held. Covering Newmarket, Halesworth, Ipswich, Mildenhall, Thetford and Colchester, Marlows brought 4,000 new customer accounts. As was usual, all the existing staff members were retained. At a stroke this gave the Ridgeons group substantially increased coverage of the region and strengthened its position against the national chains. Mildenhall, the smallest of these branches, was eventually closed. The Newmarket branch was relocated to a greenfield site, proving very successful and attracting much more custom than the nearby branch of a major rival. Halesworth, the largest, west of Southwold in Suffolk, was later moved in 2006 from its congested town centre location to a greenfield site, with a new warehouse, offices and yard. Tony Greavett, now group property director, was playing a key role in identifying and negoti-ating for these precious plots of land.

On 31 July 2000 the group purchased the business and assets of G.A. Easter in Norwich, which became the Norwich North branch. The site was typical of many of these

a bulk transport operation. Previously leased by Marlows, it was turned into a modern branch, showroom and yard, and opened as a satellite branch of Nuffield Road in 2002. This raised the total number of branches from 6 to 19 in less than five years and marked the end of the main phase of branch expansion. There were others to come. In 2007 a completely new branch was opened in May on 2 acres of land leased in Peterborough, and a new branch was opened in Pampisford, ideally situated off a junction of the A11, under the management of Keith Bane. In 2008 Ridgeons Independent Living Centre, a new venture by the group, was opened on the Pampisford site, aimed at older and disabled people requiring special equipment and home conversions to make life easier. In the same year the group also opened the Norwich South branch, the final addition before the economic crisis brought on by the near-collapse of the banking system. All the branches were linked to one or other of the main branches, Nuffield Road, Cromwell Road, March, Saffron Walden or Halesworth, which supplied the smaller branches with stock and carried out deliveries on behalf of their customers. Tony Greavett continues to keep an eagle eye open for further opportunities, for there are still gaps in the group's regional coverage, particularly in the northeast and southeast. A comprehensive branch network encourages customers to regard the group as their merchant of choice. This is accompanied by a constant review of the existing branches to ensure they remain up to date.

acquisitions, being around an acre in size, with warehousing, some 16 staff and a turnover of about £1.5m. At the same time Ridgeons also took over Wheelers Ltd, based in Sudbury. As well as operating builders' merchants in Diss and Lowestoft, Wheelers also ran a significant timber business from its 14-acre site in Sudbury. There it made roof trusses and carried out specialised work, part of which was later transferred to Herringswell. With more than 100 staff over the three sites, the business had annual sales of more than £10m. The Sudbury site in particular was large enough and ideally situated to become a distribution centre supporting the group's growing number of branches south of Saffron Walden. Noting how soon the acquisition of Wheeler's followed on from that of Easter's, David Ridgeon remarked that while the timing may not have been perfect, 'you have to take opportunities when they arise or they pass you by'.

A year later the group seized another opportunity, buying a site of more than two acres in Bury St Edmunds, formerly

Top left: Truss production and joist making (above left) at the Sudbury branch.

Above: Showroom at Ridgeons Independent Living Centre.

While branch expansion was the main thrust of the group's strategy into the new millennium, there were other changes. The opportunity to sell the Octopus stores was taken in 2000, when they were acquired by Great Mills, a national chain seeking to add to its existing four stores in the area. The wholesale distribution arm, CRS Wholesale, now under Allen Coote, continued to expand, and a third depot was opened in Derby in 2007, extending its reach into Derbyshire, Staffordshire, Nottinghamshire, the northern half of Lincolnshire and South Yorkshire. In the same year the group initiated the New Ventures programme as part of the next five-year plan. Terry Parker recalled how the programme developed from the ideas put forward by a committee that had been asked to consider ways in which the group could diversify and reduce its reliance on construction. It included the Independent Living Centre and also led to the formation of Anglia Tool Centre (ATC). Under manager Ian Thacker, ATC was set up in Bury St Edmunds in 2006, and was based entirely on sales generated from its internet website. Extending the group's existing range of power tools and promising 'next day delivery' anywhere in the UK, ATC successfully illustrated the power of the internet to eliminate geographical boundaries.

The group was already aware of the benefits of applying technology to run a more efficient business with a better focus on customer needs. Online access to customer accounts was introduced in 2002. A dedicated IT training centre was opened in Bury St Edmunds the following year. Planning was already underway for the installation of advanced management software across the group as well as a new computer system, both of which were introduced in 2008. One advantage for branch managers, through having immediate information on stock levels, was the ability to react more quickly to changing trends. Customers could order goods and receive their invoices online. What technology could not do was replace the face-to-face contact between customers, uncertain of their requirements and the price they wanted to pay, and knowledgeable sales staff in their local branch. The daily banter between customers and staff, either over the telephone or the counter, remained an important factor in building up and maintaining customer loyalty. For many customers, individual employees were the reason they did business with Ridgeons. A good example of this is Alan Stebbings, who won the Internal Salesman of the Year Recognition Award in 2007 for his service at Cromwell Road. Further enhancements to customer service came in 2000 through

Top: Staff at CRS Wholesale, Derby.

Middle left: Allen Coote, CRS Wholesale.

Middle right: Tony Greavett, who joined Ridgeons in 1973 and has

spearheaded the group's expansion project since 1997.

Bottom: Anglia Tool Centre Interior.

Above: Sales and administrative staff, Herringswell. Back row from left: Stephen Wait, Peter Wittish, Rob Sharp, John Hennessy, Terry Scripps, Paul Mazey, Graham Skillen, Phil Boston, Michael Black, Dawn Markwell, Charles Hepworth and Shirley Plume.

Below: Ridgeons Football League.

the development, under the direction of group sales manager Roger Day, of a key accounts office at Nuffield Road, which successfully led to increased sales.

Under Steve Sutton, who was now group marketing director, marketing became more sophisticated, and a marketing information system was created, helping the group to focus on specific segments of the market. More effort was invested in raising the profile of the group. After a long absence from the showground, the group began exhibiting at the Royal Norfolk Show and Suffolk Show from 2000, and trade shows were held again, at Saffron Walden and Sudbury. The group also sponsored the Eastern Counties Football League, which became known as the Ridgeon League. In 2007 the Big Blue Book, the group's first full product catalogue, was issued, a major project brought to fruition under the in-house marketing team. The group maintained an outstanding range of items in stock and, unlike many rivals, would place special orders for customers – it was said that if customers couldn't get what they wanted at Ridgeons, they couldn't get it anywhere.

Herringswell was already an impressive site, benefiting from significant investment in 1997, when a massive central yard had been set up and its capacity to produce planed and moulded timber had been increased. By the turn of the century, Herringswell was making eight million lineal metres of machined goods every year and more money was being invested in a new production line. With a million metres sold directly to the picture framing industry, the site was already exploiting its potential to serve external customers. Money was also invested in the group's timber importing operations. From 2001 Ridgeons had its own timber terminal, based on a 3-acre site at Ipswich. Under Graham Skillen, the group imported some 60,000 cubic metres of wood every year, including 20,000 cubic metres of red wood. The scale of these operations made timber a business in its own right, and it began trading as such, under the name Ridgeons Forest Products. Alan Newbury, the driving force behind this expansion, retired in 2004. Three years later, as part of the investment strategy for the timber business, Chignell Buildings Ltd, a timber frame-building firm based in Beccles, was acquired. This was done partly to provide an outlet for timber frames, I-beams and roof trusses made at the Sudbury site, where manufacturing capacity was increased. After an impassioned plea from Mike Cammack, a further major investment programme was undertaken at Herringswell. Under Alan Pealling, who became managing director of Ridgeons Forest Products in January 2008, almost £3m was spent on a new mill and new high-speed production lines, with another £2m on a new office block, warehousing and vehicles. All this, both at Sudbury and Herringswell, was completed at the beginning of 2008.

In 2004 David Ridgeon decided to step down as chairman. He was highly respected in the industry, and had

Above: David Ridgeon (centre) and Jill Ridgeon outside the Savoy Hotel, London, with his Builders' Merchant Award Lifetime Achievement award, 2003.

served as Master of the Worshipful Company of Builders' Merchants in 1999–2000. When he completed 50 years with the group in 2003, a dinner was held in his honour at Corpus Christi College in Cambridge in July. In November he attended the annual Builders' Merchant Awards for Excellence at the Savoy in London, where he received the accolade of the Lifetime Achievement award. It was fully merited. As Peter Silk had remarked at an earlier celebration in 1998 to mark David Ridgeon's 25 years as managing director and chairman: 'The pace of change quickened with David's presence. His approach to managing ran together with a deep knowledge of all aspects of builders' merchant trade; he was democratic on all decisions taken; kind, fair and considerate, and a delight to work with.' David had risen to the challenge made by his father, who had placed him in charge of Saffron Walden in his early twenties. There he had developed the approach to business that he later applied to the whole group. Although he later reflected that the way the business developed seemed rather casual in retrospect, he always had the knack of seeing the bigger picture, which gave him the confidence to seize opportunities when they arose. And he was never too afraid of risk, which he believed was an integral part of doing business. In any case, he would say, 'one of the pleasures of a private company is that you can have a go at anything'. Always fair, and seeking consensus whenever possible, David could be tough when he needed to be. For him the business was

never about ego or personal enrichment – he had to be persuaded to give up his worn-out car in exchange for a newer model. He saw himself as the latest in the family line to act as steward of the fruits achieved by those who had gone before.

David saw it as his responsibility to develop the business in a sustainable way, not only to hand over to the next generation but also to ensure the future livelihoods of those who worked for the group. As the business grew, he was happy to delegate to other senior managers and, once they had gained his trust, willing to let them take a chance on a well-argued initiative. He believed firmly in a tangible and visible link between the family, as owners of the business, and their employees. Sharing with his father and grandfather before him the core values of the business, David strove to make sure that they remained relevant and an integral part of the business as it expanded. As his brother Michael had noted on a previous occasion, 'the members of the Ridgeon family have always sought to engender a "family atmosphere" within the business and with its staff. It started with the founder, [was] developed by my father, and I know my brother David has endeavoured to continue that concept of personal concern'.

Right and below: Quality customer
service remains a key feature of
Ridgeons' ethos.

That family atmosphere was still evident in many ways, even as the group was growing. For some years there had been a Community and Social Steering Group, under the enthusiastic leadership of Jane Winney, which not only organised excursions and other events for staff, but also ran fund-raising events for national and local charities, extending the reach of the group into the wider community. By the early years of the new millennium employees were raising more than £20,000 every year. In early 2005 staff collected that sum for the appeal to relieve victims of the 2004 Boxing Day tsunami disaster. Alongside this there were still occasional day trips to France or visits to London, as well as cricket and football matches. By 2008, with almost 1,000 staff in 21 branches, three wholesale depots, three timber sites, ATC and RILP and various central support departments, a single Christmas party was no longer possible, and instead individual departments organised their own events. But the 25 Club still ran its own annual outings, dinners and Christmas parties. Special recognition was also introduced for those completing 35 years with the group. A number of staff members achieved in excess of 40 years' service, such as Dick Pinning (50 years in the March branch), John Doggett (49), Arthur Swan (49), Jack Goddard (still working part-time in 2009 after 48 years), Eddie Izard (still working as a driver in 2009 after 45 years) and Steve Lee (41). At the same time staff turnover was low, almost 60 per cent of employees had more than five years' service with the group, and the average length of service was eight years.

There are numerous instances of several generations of the same family working for the business.

There were several reasons for this. Among the other benefits enjoyed by staff were an incentive scheme, loyalty awards, staff discount and free life assurance. There was a 'Bright Ideas' scheme, as well as staff recognition awards to mark outstanding ideas and performance. They also had access to occupational health services and the opportunity to take bi-annual health checks and join a health cash plan. There was a round-the-clock confidential helpline and online service available for staff needing assistance or advice. The group also placed a great deal of importance on open discussion, consensus and support, a pattern long established under David Ridgeon. Training and development was a high priority. Learning opportunities ranged from a management development course open to anyone in the group to training on every aspect of the business, from sales and IT to products, plant and equipment. All this helped the group to achieve the Investors in People Award in 1999, winning re-accreditation in every period since. The assessor for the award remarked that 'Ridgeons [was] the John Lewis of its sector'. The very fact that the family and the senior management team together had created a successful business with the potential for further growth also encouraged staff to remain with the group.

For the group's pensioners, Linkpeople still kept in touch with them, helping the group to assist those in need wherever possible, a much-appreciated concept again derived from the personal concern fostered by the family. And, as pointed out by Dennis Stanley and Nigel Haslop, both with more than 30 years' service, many employees simply found Ridgeons a good place to work, they enjoyed the company of the people they worked with, and they were allowed to get on with their job, admittedly within more prescriptive guidelines as the business grew larger. Mainly as a result of this overall approach, the Ridgeons workforce has never been unionised.

On 1 September 2004 Anne Ridgeon, who had been appointed deputy chairman when she returned to the business in 2000, took over from her father. She was one of five family directors at the time, the others – apart from her father – being her uncle Michael, her sister Rachel and her cousin Gordon. Deeply committed to the same principles as her father, she brought from her own business experience a wider perspective and, with the support of the family, sought to make further changes to the way the group was managed so that it might benefit from best practice elsewhere. With other family members, she worked on revising the group philosophy. Issued in 2005, it began, 'In the eyes of the customer I am Ridgeons', and emphasised integrity, respect and ethics. Encouraging initiative, teamwork and continual improvement, it aspired to the creation of long-term relationships with staff, customers and suppliers, a fulfilling working environment, good career development and social responsibility in the wider community.

Anne recognised the need to equip the business for an increasingly competitive future, in which the position of independents would be under pressure from the significant

Above: Ridgeons was proud to be the first recipient of the Investors in People Award in 1994. Gillian Shepherd (centre), former cabinet minister and MP for South West Norfolk, presented the award.

Right: Staff recognition awards are given annually to mark outstanding ideas and performance. The recipients for 2010 (pictured holding their awards) are, from left: Ray Bramley, Mark Bareham, Hugh Gemmill, Martin Hurrell, Dean Crawford, Toni Martin, Dave Scarrow, Jeff Turner, Les Swann, plus representatives from the IT department, the RFP Herringswell and Sudbury Mills.

Community and Social Activities

Ridgeons has long valued the importance of fund-raising, charitable work and contributing to the local community, as well as organising social activities for staff within the group. Shown on this and facing page is a small selection of Ridgeons community and social activities.

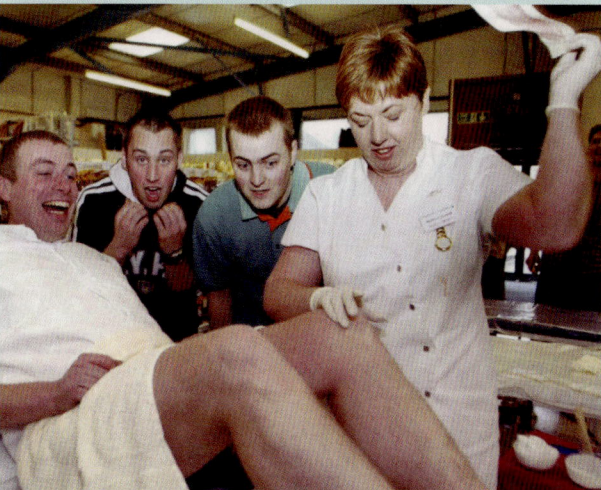

consolidation that was taking place in the industry. With help from Cranfield University, a five-year strategic plan was developed for the first time, with Anne encouraging the participation and involvement of fourth- and fifth-generation shareholders through regular shareholders' meetings.

To underpin this, Anne, with Gordon Ridgeon, drew up a proposal embodying what became known as the 'Family Purpose' – an explicit and simple definition of why the family was in business. It was intended to be, as Anne Ridgeon said, 'like a stick of rock – wherever you cut the business in the future, the experience would always be the same'. This proposal met with rapid and universal approval since it met everyone's understanding of the purpose of the business. Everyone concurred that, in Anne's words, 'the company provides us with the best means to make a difference – to people and the local communities in which we live and do business'. The key principles were distilled as

Extra-Ordinary Customer Service
Extra-Ordinary Employment
Extra-Ordinary Good Citizenship

There was ambition to expand the group to secure a sustainable business providing employment for many people and their families and benefiting the wider community; but the drivers of growth had to be balanced against the need to fund the sustainable achievement of the Family Purpose and maintain the culture that has been an integral part of Ridgeon's success.

There were other advantages to making the purpose of the business explicit. Against the backdrop of approaches from the trade to purchase Ridgeons, and with the impending retirement of Terry Parker, the family had to be clear about what it expected from his successor as managing director, particularly in terms of management style and values. And since the scale of the group, with 27 sites and more than a thousand employees, prevented the family from being as close to their employees as previous generations had been, it was imperative to find alternative ways of ensuring that the family's ethos and priorities remained at the core of the business.

To provide the security of the long-term sustainability of the business, Anne Ridgeon also reformed the corporate governance of the group, seeking to achieve the right balance between active and involved family ownership and the very capable executives sharing the family's ethics and aspirations. An executive board was created, separate from the full board, with clear guidelines for those decisions

reserved to the family. With some initial reluctance from directors, the group's first externally appointed non-executive directors were recruited from 2007. Tony Williams, a former director of Tarmac, was succeeded in April 2008 by Frank Attwood, the former senior partner of the group's auditors, and David Sarti, the chief operating officer of Marshalls plc, a major supplier to the group. For Anne Ridgeon, the group was 'privileged to have David and Frank, whose outside business experience has enabled us to look increasingly outside the confines of the group and draw so quickly upon best governance practice elsewhere'.

When Terry Parker retired in 2008, the group recruited for the first time a new group managing director who, although experienced in the industry, had never been previously associated with Ridgeons. Angela Rushforth took up her post on 1 June 2008. She had spent several years with Screwfix before joining Wolseley plc as UK marketing director in 2005. Soon afterwards, another key post was also filled in the same way, when Chris Greaves became group director for human resources. At the same time, recently appointed group directors promoted from within the business included David Bryan, the operations director, and Tony Greavett, the property director, while Nick Sims, the sales and purchasing director, was recruited from BSS.

When Angela Rushforth joined the group, she found Ridgeons to be 'distinctly different'. She was impressed by the excellent customer service and product displays she found in the branches, which contrasted favourably with many of its rivals. She also found there was 'a sense that people cared about the business'. During her first three months, she visited every branch, met every branch manager, as well as customers and suppliers, and received a very positive impression. She was struck by how staff members were receptive to the need for change, even if this caused some degree of anxiety.

It was a difficult time for the new managing director to take over. The group had performed well as it grew during the previous decade. In 1997 Ridgeons achieved a turnover of nearly £65m with net profits of £2.1m; by 2004, sales had exceeded £112m, and improved margins produced net profits of £7.9m. The Cambridge and Saffron Walden branches remained the largest contributors, with their sales dwarfing the contributions achieved by the typical branches operated by national chains. But economic conditions began to deteriorate from the beginning of 2008, steadily worsening as the year progressed. While the revenue earned by the branches fell, the downturn particularly affected the timber business, where the multi-million pound investment in new capacity was just coming on stream.

The impact of the previous recession during the early 1990s, when so many employees had lost their jobs, had reinforced the determination of the family to prevent this from happening again if at all possible. Indeed, during the late 1990s, when many national operators were still laying off staff to improve margins, Ridgeons consciously resisted the idea. So the strategy employed as the new recession took effect was based on immediate cost savings as an indication of tough times ahead, such as a freeze on vacancies, coupled with the identification of further reductions other than staff-related expenditure. Only then was an assessment made of the possible savings available from cutting back on staff – but even then this was planned on the basis of the group breaking even.

By the autumn of 2008 it was clear that the deepening recession would mean job cuts, and an announcement was made that up to 95 jobs would have to go in January the following year. In the event, 78 staff members were laid off, of which 38 were voluntary redundancies. This had to be followed in the summer of 2009 by another 35 job losses, reducing the group's workforce to just over 800. Ridgeons was not alone within the sector in taking such drastic action but this did little to ease the pain for all those involved. The group was determined to ensure that those involved received every support both during and after the process. Retraining sessions were offered and the group kept in contact with those who left. The scale of the job losses deeply affected every family member for, as Anne Ridgeon remarked, 'we've always been obsessive about how we care for our staff'. She visited every member of staff under threat of redundancy and apologised to them.

At the same time the opportunity was taken to further rebalance the way the group was managed. There had been a tendency as the group expanded and developed for divisions within the group to act as separate organisations, which created inconsistencies as a result. The reorganisation of the senior management team redressed this, with group directors acting on behalf of the whole Ridgeons group, rather than particular parts of the business. This approach also began to percolate downwards, so, for instance, ATC catalogues became available within every branch. Among the changes was the appointment of a new group finance director, Ian Northen, while Rachel Anderson, David's elder daughter, relinquished her non-executive role in favour of her cousin, and Gordon Ridgeon's sister, Amanda Ridgeon.

The action taken by the group in difficult circumstances, together with its traditional strengths – depth and breadth of stock, customer service and the knowledge, loyalty and expertise of staff – as well as a prudent financial approach, ensured that Ridgeons retained its core customer base in the face of fierce competition from rivals and even gained new customers. This was intended to place the group in an advantageous position when the first signs of an economic recovery began to appear.

As Ridgeons approaches its centenary in 2011, the business remains true to the philosophy of its founder. It continues to adhere to high standards of ethics, probity and management. For Ridgeons, corporate social responsibility, now a fashionable phrase, is nothing new; it has always been part of the way the group has operated. Established, largely through the leadership shown by David Ridgeon, as the leading business of its type in East Anglia, Ridgeons is uninterested in becoming so big that its traditions are diluted. It aims to consolidate its regional position, while seeking further appropriate diversification, in order to create a sustainable business in which the family remains central to safeguarding its ethos and character. As Anne Ridgeon has remarked, the business is 'written into the fabric of our family … it expresses who we are as a family'.

Anne and David Ridgeon toast Terry Parker's retirement, 2008. Terry had worked for Ridgeons for 37 years. From left: Angela Rushforth, Terry Parker, Anne Ridgeon and David Ridgeon.

Members of Ridgeon Group Staff *

Christopher Abbot	Russell Baird	Alan Benson-Nutt	Kevin Brinkley	Roger Cameron	Martin Codling
David Adams	Kenneth Baker	Michael Bentinck	Vincent Brinkley	Daniel Cammack	Stuart Coe
Jonathan Adams	Kevin Baker	Emma Bentley	Darren Bristow	Michael Cammack	Alfred Cole
Chantel Adcock	Mervyn Baker	Ian Bentley	Simon Broadhurst	Andrew Campbell	Brian Cole
Brian Agnew	Patricia Baker	Louise Bentley	Derek Bromage	-Sturgess	Denise Colella
Sally Akehurst	Shaun Balaam	Ronald Bentley	Keith Brook	Donald Cannon	Carl Collins
Michael Alabaster	Philip Baldry	Jonathan Betts	Peter Brook	Sandra Carlton	Nicola Collins
Stephen Alda	Adrian Ball	Yvonne Beukes	Lynda Brooks	James Carr	Robert Collins
Keith Alderton	Cheryl Bandorski	Gavin Bickers	Kirk Broom	Paul Carter	Martin Connolly
Jason Aldous	Kieth Bane	David Biggs	Richard Brothwell	Paul Caruana	Ashley Connor
Gary Aldred	Paul Bane	Steven Binks	Andrew Brown	Robert Carvell	Steven Connor
Carol Allen	David Barber	John Binns	Charles Brown	Terence Cass	Barrie Cook
Clive Allen	Debra Barber	Bertie Bird	Lesley Brown	Sam Cassidy	Dale Cook
Dawn Allen	Jean Barber	Cheri Bird	Malcolm Brown	Steven Cator	Daniel Cook
Lee Allen	Mark Barber	Trevor Bivens	Rebecca Brown	David Cattermole	David Cook
Shaun Allgood	Heather Barcroft	Daniel Black	Robin Brown	Simon Cavie	Denise Cook
James Allison	Mark Bareham	Michael Black	Stuart Brown	Karen Chandler	Terence Cook
Paul Ames	Michael Barham	Jason Blackmore	Simon Browning	Brian Chaplin	Howard Cooke
Justin Ames	James Barker	Peter Blades	David Bruce	Annette Chapman	Neil Cooke
Keith Anderson	Steven Barker	Michael Block	David Bryan	Denise Chapman	Paul Cooke
Terence Anderton	Robert Barnes	Janet Blount	Phillip Bryant	Graham Chapman	Carol Cooper
Elaine Andrew	Neil Barr	Alan Blower	Liam Brydon	Philip Chapman	Gavin Cooper
John Andrews	Stuart Barratt	Mark Bolton	Linda Bryne	Steven Charles	Ian Cooper
Raymond Andrus	Robert Barrett	Kevin Borein	David Buck	Robert Chase	Matthew Cooper
Caroline Annetts	Nicholas Barritt	David Boston	Geoffrey Buckingham	Agustin Chichon	Allen Coote
Richard Ansell	Jarrod Barton	Philip Boston	Raymond Buckingham	Martin Chubb	Nicholas Coppins
Paul Archer	Trevor Barwood	Jenna Boud	Keith Bunn	Daniel Clark	Jennifer Corden
Paul Arndt	Colin Bateman	Bradley Boughton	Penelope Bunn	Jonathan Clark	James Cornish
Antony Arnold	Peter Batterbee	Simon Boulby	Ryan Bunn	Michelle Clark	Christine Cottell
Gary Arnold	Peter Baxter	Edwin Bowen	Jennifer Burgess	Paul Clark	Graham Cotterill
Steven Arnold	Audrey Bazeley	David Bower	Donna Burkin	Darren Clarke	Paul Coulson
Steven Arrowsmith	Kevan Beavis	Rosalyn Bowkis	Alison Burton	Geoffrey Clarke	Robert Courtney
Matthew Arthurton	John Beck	Mark Boyes	Allan Burton	Ian Clarke	Nuno Coutinho
Nicola Ashforth	Laurence Beer	Alistair Brace	James Burton	Stephen Clarke	Roger Cox
Lee Atterbury	Richard Belcher	Raymond Bramley	James Burton	Mark Clay	Patricia Coxhill
Daniel Austin	Ben Bellward	Stuart Brasnett	David Butcher	Neil Clay	Stephen Cracknell
Peter Avery	James Benn	Andrew Breed	Mark Butcher	Margaret Clayton	Dean Crawford
Amanda Ayres	Geoffrey Bennett	Wayne Brett	Bob Butler	Neil Clayton	Heather Crick
Adam Bacon	George Bennett	Garry Bridges	Clifford Butler	Alison Clements	Mathew Crighton
Vincent Badcock	Linda Bennett	Abigail Briggs	Ian Butler	David Closs	Robin Croft
Alex Bagnall	Gregory Benson	Christine Briggs	Katrina Cainzos-Sola	David Coates	Martin Cross
John Bagot	Mark Benson	Shane Brignell	Derrick Cameron	Paul Cockerill	Melanie Cross

Adam Cullum	Shaun Durrant	Paul Flood	David Greenhill	Jennifer Hewish	Mark Hutchings
Andrew Cummins	Andrew Dyer	Marc Flower	Clive Griggs	Adam Hewitt	Kim Hutley
Mark Cunningham	Kevin Eagle	Michael Forwood	Louise Groves	Diane Hewitt	Barry Ibbs
Terence Cutter	Judy Eaglen	Andrew Foster	Michael Groves	John Hewitt	Aaron Iddiols
Brian Daglish	Nicholas Easter	Peter Fox	Corinne Gula	Ross Hewitt	Steven Iddiols
Stephen Dale	Craig Eastwood	Roy Frary	Tony Gunner	Shane Hicks	Robert Illsley
Emma Daniels	Marcel Eaves	Ian Frazer	Hugh Guntrip	Anne Higley	Charles Izard
Mark Daniels	Owen Eden	Jean Freeman	Dennis Guy	Dennis Hill	Barrie Jackson
Ian Danks	Arthur Edgeworth	Brian Fretwel	Neil Hagget	Michael Hill	Steven Jackson
Donna Davies	Ronald Edwards	Christopher Frost	Trevor Halls	Ian Hills	David Jacobs
Jamie Davis	Stephen Edwards	Paul Fuller	Kevin Hamer	Neil Hilsden	Simon Jarvis
Richard Dawe	Terence Edwards	Colin Galbraith	Christopher Hamill	Scott Hilsden	Samuel Jefford
Brian Day	Susan Eglen	John Gale	Karli Hammond	Peter Hilton	Steven Jeggo
Eric Day	Marc Eldred	Stephen Gale	Robin Hammond	Glen Hindmarsh	Roger Jenkins
Roger Day	Stuart Elkins	David Galloway	David Hardy	Graham Hitter	Tony Jepp
Christopher Deacon	Sandra Ellingham	Mark Gardiner	Mark Hardy	Tony Hoad	Nigel Jillings
Jason Dear	Peter Ellis	Trevor Garwood	David Hare	Jane Hobson	Derek Johnson
Judith Dempsey	Garry Ellis	Christopher Gavin	Simon Hare	James Hogan	Mark Johnson
Joseph Dennis	Gavin Emery	Hugh Gemmill	John Harford	Roger Holland	Peter Johnson
Timothy Densham	Catherine Evans	David George	Brian Harman	Carol Hollick	Stephen Johnson
Robert De Roy	Neville Evans	Peter George	David Harmer	Steven Holliday	Stuart Johnson
Steven Dethridge	Robert Evans	Peter George	Dean Harper	Richard Hollidge	Richard Jolley
Paul Dewey	Stephen Evans	David Gibson	Maxwell Harris	Richard Hollings	David Jolly
John Dicken	Zerin Fairbanks-Gilbert	Ben Giddings	Melanie Harris	Alan Holmes	Donna Jolly
Paul Ding	Amanda Fane	Benjamin Gilbert	David Harrison	Patrick Holwill	Barry Jones
Peter Dobson	Nicholas Farr	Linda Gilbert	Adrian Harvey	Sam Horgan	Candice Jones
Margaret Doggett	Andrew Featherstone	Stephen Giles	Anthony Harvey	Clive Hornsby	Clayton Jones
Simon Donaldson	Gary Feeney	Daniel Gillings	Michael Harvey	Michael Horton	David Jones
Robert Dorking	Darren Feltham	Shaun Girling	Stuart Harvey	Paul Houlden	Keith Jones
Roy Doubleday	Audovin Fenn	John Glaister	Nigel Haslop	Leslie How	Paul Jones
Joe Douglas	Jason Fenn	Laurence Glaister	Alexander Hassapladakis	Christopher Howard	Peter Jones
David Downes	Cristina Fernandes	Adam Goddard	David Hastings	Anthony Howe	David Jordan
Graham Downey	Mary Fernandez	Jack Goddard	Iain Hastings	Darren Howe	Pawel Jozefowicz
Christopher Doyle	David Fields	Karl Goddard	Craig Hawes	Kane Howgego	Adrian Julings
Timothy Draper	Michael Fields	Kerry Golding	Paul Hayden	Luke Howgego	Randy Kalume
Gillian Draycott	William Fields	Gary Good	Adrian Hayes	Max Howgego	David Keen
Amanda Drew	Richard Fincham	Wesley Goodchild	Mark Hayland	Robert Howgego	Martin Keen
Melissa Drew	Phillip Firman	Ben Gorham	Malcolm Hayward	Dale Huckle	Wayne Keen
David Drewery	Tracy Fisher	Mark Gossington	Nicola Hayward	Matthew Hudson	David Kennedy
David Dring	Brian Fitzgerald	Roger Graham	Ian Hedges	Adam Hughes	Richard Kent
Ivan Drury	Mark Fitzhenry	Valerie Graham	Clifford Hellmers	Brian Hughes	Ryan Kent
Christine Duffy	Kayne Fletcher	Peter Gray	Andrew Henderson	David Hunnable	Martyn Kenworthy
Jonathan Dunckley	Martin Fletcher	Scott Gray	Scott Henn	Nicholas Hunn	Edward Keogh
Jonathan Dunkley	Nicholas Flint	Chris Greaves	John Hennessy	Simon Hunt	Robert Ketteridge
Christopher Dunn	Karl Flintoff	Anthony Greavett	Belinda Henocq	Ewan Hunter	Nicholas Keymer
Christopher Dunsmure	Maureen Flintoff	David Green	Charles Hepworth	Martin Hurrell	Neil Kimber
Anthony Durose	Derrin Flood	Neil Green	Chris Herrell	Christopher Hutchings	Emma King

Anita Kirk	Jeremy Lugg	Stephen Mcdermott	Malcolm Nash	Nathan Peachey	David Richards
Kevin Klimowicz	Leon Macdonald	Timothy Mcdermott	Thomas Nash	Andrew Peacock	Simon Richards
Paul Knight	Darren Mace	Nicholas McFarlane	Gary Naven	Martin Peacock	Robert Riches
John Knights	Philip Mace	Julie Mclernon	Melissa Neal	Stuart Peacock	Ivan Riddleston
Pawel Kukula	Glen Macer	Derek Mcpeak	Sarah Needham	Alan Pealling	Anne Ridgeon
George Kyle	David Mackenzie	Richard Mead	Nicholas Neill	Dawn Pearce	Gordon Ridgeon
Kevin Kyle	Nicholas Mackenzie	Hazel Meadows	Douglas Neville	Gary Pearce	Martin Ringham
Matthew Lacey	Margaret Maclean	Jason Mealing	John Newell	Wayne Pearce	Mark Ripley
Nathan Lake	Simon Maddams	Julian Medcalf	Nigel Newell	Andrew Peat	Alison Roberts
Matthew Lancaster	Radoslaw Makowski	Tony Merrell	Stephanie Newell	Malcolm Peel	Carol Roberts
Jennifer Lane	David Mallindine	Peter Merry	Margaret Newland	Sarah Pegg	David Roberts
Ian Larter	Gerald Mann	Paul Middleton	Richard Newland	Gareth Percival	John Roberts
Christopher Laurie	Gurkinder Mann	Shane Middleton	Ian Newman	Steven Percival	Gary Robertson
Claire Lawrence	David Mannell	Alan Miles	Jodie Newman	Jenna Perrin	Louise Robertson
Lesley Lawrence	Patrick Manning	Alan Millard	Mark Newman	Andrew Peters	Michael Robins
Dean Lawson	Michael Mannion	Kenneth Miller	Gary Nichols	Benjamin Phillips	John Robinson
Paul Leczycki	Roy Mansell	Gary Miller	Ian Nightingale	Michael Phillips	Chris Rodger
Calvin Lee	Mark Mansfield	Jacqueline Miller	Steven Nixon	Nicholas Phillips	Guy Rodgers
Rodney Lee	Paul Manton	Sidney Miller	Laurence Nolan	Stephen Phillips	Ian Roe
Katherine Lee Own	David Markham	Steven Miller	Ian Northen	Terence Phillips	Christian Rogers
Colin Lefevre	Brett Marks	Reginald Mills	James Norton	Daniel Piasecki	Paul Rogers
Cadell Lench	Dawn Markwell	Jon Milnes	David Nunn	Amy Pigott	William Rogers
Shane Lennon	Amy Marlow	Brian Minns	John Oman	Stephen Pilsworth	Sharon Rohn
Elaine Lenton	Glyn Marsden	Michael Minns	Steven O'Neil	Gary Pipe	Jaroslaw Roj
Jonathan Lester	Matthew Marsden	Raymond Minns	David Osborn	Katie Pitchford	Jenny Rudd
Benjamin Levett	Darrin Marsh	Jane Miranda	Andrew Outlaw	Terry Plappert	Shane Rudland
Adam Lewis	Richard Marsh	Ewa Misiak	Kiran Padhiar	Peter Pleasance	Elliott Rumens
Robert Lewis	Cheryl Martin	Helen Mitchell	Jamie Page	Donna Pledger	Paul Ryan
Alexander Limpus	Craig Martin	Selma-Louis Mitchell	Michael Page	Shirley Plume	James Salmons
Julie Lindsay	Katie Martin	Richard Mobberley	Alan Palmer	Samuel Potter	Harry Samkin
Philip Lindsay	Peter Martin	David Moller	Colin Palmer	Paul Poulter	Christopher Sampson
Matthew Ling	Toni Martin	Jane Monk	Jeanette Palmer	David Poulton	Amanda Sandercock
Francilina Liston	Rebecca Mason	John Monk	Richard Palmer	Andrew Price	Denese Sapsford
Michael Littlechild	John Mason	Charles Moore	Roy Papworth	Roberta Price	David Sayer
James Littlewood	Peter Mason	Clare Moore	Terry Parker	Paul Proudler	Greg Scarrott
Gary Liversage	Shaun Mason	Jeremy Moore	Robert Parkinson	Ricky Pyke	David Scarrow
Mark Liversage	Elin Massey	Richard Moore	Mohammad Parkook	Mandy Ramsbottom	Susan Schneider
Valerie Lloyd	Derek Masters	Frances Morgan	Imma Parlato	Michael Ramsbottom	David Scraggs
Matthew Locke	Allan Matthews	Robert Mortimer	Andrew Parrish	Michael Randall	Terrence Scripps
Suzanne Lomas	Anthony Matthews	John Mortlock	Ian Pass	Martin Reed	Priscilla Scroggie
Andrew Longhurst	Neil Matthews	Valerie Morton	Diane Pateman	Nicholas Rees	Keith Seager-Myers
Kevin Longman	Hans May	Nicholas Moss	Stephen Pavitt	Michelle Reeve	Alan Seamark
Kelvin Lord	Andrew Mazey	William Mount	Simon Pawley	Edward Reeves	Adam Searing
Arthur Loveday	Paul Mazey	Karl Moyes	Peter Paxton	Peter Remnant	Anthony Seddon
Julie Lucas	David Mcarthur	Ivor Muncey	Katherine Payne	Anthony Revens	Owen Seeley
Nicholas Luck	Michael Mccaffrey	Andrew Munden	Andrew Peach	Adam Rhodes	Joseph Selby
Steven Luckman	Marion Mccormack	Matthew Mynott	Terry Peacher	Christopher Rice	Steven Sellick

Andrew Sewell	Claire St Ledger	Arthur Swan	Christopher Tracey	Paul Watson	Andrew Wilson
Stephen Sewell	Paul Stalker	Barry Swann	Gwendoline Traveller	Keith Weavers	Martin Wilson
Sarah Seymour	Dennis Stanley	Leslie Swann	Simon Trimnell	Alan Webb	Robert Wilson
Stuart Shadbolt	Justin Stanworth	Alan Symonds	Ian Truelove	Claire Webb	Sam Wilson
Malcolm Shanks	Michael Stapleton	Aaron Tabbanor	Christian Tryc	Daniel Webb	Andrew Winfield
Robin Sharp	Barry Start	Anthony Tatum	Peter Tubby	David Webb	Jane Winney
Timothy Shave	David Stearn	Claire Taylor	James Turner	Graham Weeks	Peter Wittish
Ian Shaw	Philip Stearn	Lauren Taylor	Jeffrey Turner	Christopher Weet	Daniel Wojciechowski
Katherine Shearing	Alan Stebbings	Simon Taylor	Matthew Upchurch	Brian Wells	Rafal Wolski
Michael Shepherd	Mark Stevens	Ian Thacker	Shaun Utting	Lilian Wells	Deborah Wood
Sally Sherman	Neil Stevens	Samuel Thake	Stephen Vale	Robert Wesson	John Wood
Peter Sievewright	Derek Steventon	Mark Thomas	David Verlander	Fahad Weston	Vincent Woods
Lawrence Simmons	Hilary Stiff	Raymond Thomas	Damien Vickers	Julie Weston	David Woolley
Victoria Simms	Trevor Still	Trevor Thomas	Fiona Viney	Martin Weston	Vicki Woolnough
Gillian Simpson	Gary Stinton	Adam Thompson	Pamela Voutt	Adrian Westwood	Mark Wordingham
Nick Sims	David Stocker	Caroline Thompson	David Wade	Graham Wheeler	Denise Wreathall
Steve Sinclair	Matthew Stocker	Colin Thompson	Ian Waine	Michael Wheeler	Jenna Wright
Justin Singletary	Rachel Stockley	Ryan Thompson	Annette Wait	Matt Whitby	Mark Wright
John Sismey	Rhonda Stokes	Ann Thomson	Stephan Wait	Scott Whitby	Raymond Wright
Graham Skillen	Kevin Storey	Emma Thorne	Christopher Walker	Michael Whitwell	Richard Wright
Alan Smith	Kevin Strangward	Charles Thorogood	Douglas Wallace	Timothy Wigby	Robert Wright
Antony Smith	Zowie Straughan	Walter Thorrington	Mark Walrond	Krissy Wild	Emma Wyatt
David Smith	Gary Stroud	James Thurbin	Yvonne Walrond	Aaron Williams	Mary Yates
Emma Smith	Daniel Sturman	Daniel Timmons	John Walsh	Andrew Williams	Andrew Yeoman
Gareth Smith	Maurice Sturman	Antony Timms	Gareth Ward	Calum Williams	Alan Young
Garry Smith	Merle Sturt	Nicholas Tingey	Nicola Ward	Carl Williams	John Young
Graham Smith	James Suddery	Darren Tobyn	Raymond Ward	David Williams	Mark Young
Martin Smith	Danny Sullivan	Matthew Tofts	Beryl Wardley	Joel Williams	Susan Young
Matthew Smith	Paul Sulman	Allan Tomlinson	Timothy Warnock	Melvyn Williams	Andrew Youngman
Roland Smith	Douglas Sutherland	Daryl Tooke	Danielle Watcham	Robert Williams	Matthew Youngman
Raymond Snell	Nathan Suttle	Ian Tosh	Susan Waters	Andrew Williamson	Krzysztof Zaluski
Sean Spaxman	Steven Sutton	Desmond Townsend	Graham Waterson	Jennifer Willis	Lynn Zarattini
Michael Spray	Emma Swallowe	Stephen Townsend	Andrew Watkins	Steven Willis	Nicholas Zarkos

*Those members employed in 2008 and as at 30 June 2010.

25 Club Past and Present Members

Past and Present Members with 25 Years Service or More**

Present Members

P R Silk Sept 1937	G Rowlandson Feb 1966	R Maynard Nov 1975
R J Nunn June 1940	J P Williams Aug 1966	P Merry Feb 1976*
G E Smith July 1944	A J Davis Aug 1967	R Belcher Aug 1976
R T Langford Aug 1944	S Lee Sept 1967	J Mortlock Aug 1976
H C Carter Aug 1947	M Stock June 1968	N Jillings Nov 1976
R J A Doggett Sept 1950	A Locke July 1968	D Markham Aug 1977
Miss M Andrews May 1952	W J Shepherd Feb 1969	M Littlechild Sept 1977
D C E Ridgeon Jan 1953	B L Flower Apr 1970	K Bane Feb 1978
T J Belcher July 1953	G P Stinton Nov 1970	I Drury Feb 1978
B R C Ashby Oct 1954	R Ketteridge Apr 1971	A Kent July 1978
R D Coleman Aug 1956	A Seddon May 1971	T Newman July 1978
K H Sweeney Oct 1956	P Hutt May 1971	K Miller Aug 1978
J M Cox July 1957	N Haslop Aug 1971	C Bateman Oct 1978
E Page Mar 1958	A Webb Aug 1971	J Agate Dec 1978
A Davey Mar 1958	I Muncey Apr 1972	P Rogers Nov 1979
R Pottrill Mar 1958	A Blower June 1972	R Bentley Nov 1979
A W Thompson Mar 1958	A Coote June 1972	P Middleton Feb 1980
P Young Mar 1958	A Rowlandson Aug 1972	A Stebbings Apr 1980
J F Hawkins Oct 1958	Mrs M Evans Dec 1972	C Duffy May 1980
D M Powell May 1959	S Arrowsmith Jan 1973	A Peach June 1980
R A Curtis Sept 1959	Mrs L Carter Feb 1973	S Allgood July 1980
A Swan Apr 1960	D Hunnable Mar 1973	P Sievewright July 1979*
J G Williams Feb 1961	A Greavett Apr 1973	Mrs V Storey May 1981
J Goddard May 1961	M Symons June 1973	P Bryant Sept 1981
R Hughes Jan 1962	T Cutter July 1973	P Stearn Sept 1981
G F Markham Mar 1962	Mrs M Smith May 1967*	G Benson Oct 1981
S E Garrett Mar 1962	Miss A Thomson Oct 1973	S Gale Mar 1982
R G R Andrus Nov 1962	M Chapman Apr 1974	D Jolly Mar 1982
S Wityk Apr 1963	N Moss Aug 1974	M Brown Oct 1982*
B W Symonds Apr 1963	A Young Nov 1974	S Dale May 1983
R M Wright June 1963*	M Shanks Dec 1974	J Hewitt May 1983
P C Lawrence Apr 1964	D Stanley Apr 1975	D Stearn June 1983
H Cranwell Apr 1964	S Miller May 1975	A Symonds June 1983
E Izard June 1964	J Sismey June 1973*	C Webb June 1983
P Baker Aug 1964	M Wheeler July 1975	S Willis June 1983
I J Saunders Jan 1965	S Marchment Aug 1975	R Butler Aug 1983
C S Lee Aug 1965	G Stroud Oct 1975	R Day Sept 1983
T Parker Nov 1965*	R Mills Oct 1975	P Gray Oct 1983

J Lester Oct 1983

G Ridgeon Oct 1983

P Cockerill Nov 1983

R Fincham Nov 1983

D Scarrow Nov 1983

R Jolley Dec 1983

T Draper Feb 1984

S Hare Jan 1984

D Harrison Nov 1984

T Merrell Jan 1984

N Newell June 1984

B Wardley Mar 1984

V Woods July 1984

S Sutton Jan 1984

J Winney July 1984

R Ansell Dec 1984*

S Schneider Sept 1984

G Bennett Feb 1985

D Marsh Feb 1985

M Shepherd Mar 1985

J Dicken July 1985

K Golding July 1985

K Alderton Aug 1985

J Eaglen Dec 1985

Past Members

Cyril Ridgeon Apr 1911–Jan 1942

W J Cornell Apr 1912–Nov 1955

L W Ridgeon May 1913–Jan 1981

W Cullum Unknown 1913–Apr 1955

S Stone May 1919–Dec 1971

C Elliot Ridgeon Apr 1920–July 1973

J Stone Aug 1921–June 1950

J H Rivers Feb 1922–June 1971

C Smith Sept 1922–Dec 1973

J Jarman June 1923–June 1987

C Briant Nov 1925–Nov 1975

S Haynes May 1926–Oct 1964

K Stone Mar 1927–May 1974

L Bigmore June 1928–Feb 1979

B James Aug 1928–Aug 1977

P Moule Feb 1929–Aug 1958

R Parkinson Mar 1929–Jan 1986*

R Rolfe June 1929–Jan 1982

A Chapman June 1929–June 1983

W Naylor July 1929–Aug 1979

V Setchell Sept 1929–Sept 1996

P L Cox Dec 1929–June 2003

V Keys Mar 1930–Aug 1985

W T Feakes June 1930–May 2000

W J Clarke July 1930–Mar 1991

Mrs B Ridgeon Jan 1931–Sept 1966

Mrs Elliot Ridgeon Jan 1931–Aug 1993

I E Warren Oct 1931–Jan 1998

W Batterbee May 1932–Nov 1978

A R Butler May 1932–Oct 1991

R Kitson Apr 1933–Oct 1998

F Dean Sept 1934–Mar 2001

A Coulson Oct 1934–Nov 1989

Mrs W Davies Oct 1935–Feb 1982

S C Palmer Oct 1937–Feb 2000

D Williams Mar 1938–Sept 2001

A Corn July 1939–Oct 1976

K Chalkley Apr 1940–Dec 1981

R J W Cornell Oct 1940–May 1979

Mrs J Nunn Feb 1942–Jan 2004*

F W Ashberry July 1942–Dec 1988

M C Rowell Aug 1942–May 2001

C W Tavener Sept 1942–June 1999*

P R Marshall Sept 1943–Nov 1992

A E Bowyer Oct 1945–Jan 1992

J Anderson Nov 1945–Aug 2009

J T Reed Nov 1945–Aug 1978

H G Richards Nov 1945–May 1997

R J Martin Apr 1945–Sept 2009

B R Hawkins Mar 1946–Apr 1977

J J Ross Oct 1946–May 1981

R Soulsby Nov 1946–Dec 1987

R K Rush Nov 1946–May 1989

R W Hunter Dec 1946–Dec 1972

B Smith May 1948–Aug 1984

R Abbs Aug 1948–Oct 1995

C Utteridge Oct 1948–Dec 1976

A E Hall Oct 1949–Mar 1999

E C Francis July 1950–Jan 1977

W G Poulter Apr 1951–Aug 1987

T H Flatt Apr 1952–May 2000

C V Lindsay Jan 1953–Oct 2009

Mrs Y Fordham Sept 1954–Oct 2007

W Barker Mar 1958–Mar 1995

E C Wells Mar 1958–May 2000

L Camp Mar 1958–June 2000

C R Porter Mar 1958–Sept 1997

A Wrankmore Mar 1958–Oct 1999

A Ridgewell Mar 1958–Feb 1988

H King Mar 1958–June 1987

R D Pinning Aug 1958–May 2008

A F Chandler Sept 1958–June 2004

J E Hobbs Jan 1960–Oct 1995

N A Bacon Aug 1960–Aug 2002

E Smith Dec 1963–Mar 2001

F G Mansfield Jan 1967–Apr 2008

Mrs P Pagram Mar 1971–Mar 2009

Mrs E Knott June 1972–Dec 2005

B Gray Feb 1974–Aug 1999

T Harmon May 1978–Sept 2007

R Coxall Unknown–May 2008

* Broken Service

** details correct as at 8 October 2010.

Index

Illustrations are denoted in bold. Streets, colleges etc without a named location are in Cambridge.